Johnny Walters is a male, born in Ghana on November 14, 1958. He came to Denmark in 1979, and has been a citizen since 1988. He has been a partner in a business company, since 1992, working as an International Broker in Trade, Finance, and Services, which has contributed to his many travels around the world due mainly to his international business relations. He has four children from previous relationships, and is currently single.

I dedicate this book to the suffering and voiceless people on, and from, the African continent.

Johnny Walters

"AFRICA" –
DOOMED?

AUSTIN MACAULEY PUBLISHERS™

LONDON • CAMBRIDGE • NEW YORK • SHARJAH

A CIP catalogue record for this title is available from the British Library.

ISBN 9781788481397 (Paperback)
ISBN 9781788481403 (Hardback)
ISBN 9781788481410 (E-Book)
www.austinmacauley.com

First Published (2018)
Austin Macauley Publishers Ltd™
25 Canada Square
Canary Wharf
London
E14 5LQ

Contents

Quoting the lyrics from my song:

"But How"

"You've got the rain, the moon, the stars above,
You've got the sun; you've even got the snow,
You've got the land, the greens, the seas on earth,
You've got the gold; you even got the blue skies,
But tell me how: how can it go so wrong?

You've got a life and all the love with it,
You've got a name, you also got a way of life that you
live,
You are a man; you've got the means in you to make it
work,
You've also got the right to life in harmony,
So tell me: how can it be so bad?

You have seen things you should not see,
You have done things should not be done,
Let your kindness NOT be a weakness,
Lift up your eyes and look above, there's hope in life if
you care to see,
It's a shame though it should be this way, in need of help
and none in sight."

Preface

"Africa, Africa, Africa!" So familiar a name but I cannot deny, and ignore the very simple fact that it sounds easy, common, and inviting to say. One can actually get used to this name as the name is an abstract reflection of so many things; mystical, weird, exotic, degradation, suffering, hunger, and all other strange and mixed pictures popping up in one's head.

With this book, I am attempting to create a debate and stir awareness to what I consider the most unfair deliberate or non-deliberate efforts to keep a whole society from experiencing and enjoying the full potential that should be available to every human being and society on this earth.

I have much more than often wondered what the name "Africa" stands for. What does this name mean or represent, and why this name more than often spells only negativity. As clearly as I can remember to this day, I have for a quite number of years seriously wondered why I automatically expect some form of negative information or news when the name "Africa" is either mentioned or appears in a written form. I can remember the many frustrations I have experienced just by hearing or seeing this name – "Africa".

Why, why and how is this so? I will frequently ask myself. Is this really true? Can this be true? In everyday life, social, cultural and sports contexts, the name "Africa" has a condescending tone to it. As a matter of fact, I have been jokingly wondering whether when there is any positive reference made about the world in the news media or otherwise, that the continent of Africa and its citizens do at all feature in the minds of those by whom those references are made. The big rock bands having a world tour, a sports event somewhere, the news anchorman or woman who is presenting some interesting information about the world, the paper media writing about an interesting or informative event taking place or have taken place somewhere outside the continent of Africa. Do they really truly consider the African continent as part of the world reference? I ask.

Is it on purpose that the continent of Africa is systematically misrepresented? Why is North Africa often referred to as the Middle East? Is Africa a country of a particular looking people? Is an African person stereotyped? Why do the international media and community as a whole make references to the African continent as a country with one group of people with one language? 'An African dance', 'An African-looking man or woman', 'An African food or cuisine', An African this or that', but I very seldom hear 'A European this or that', or 'A South American or an Asian this or that...'. This observation is remarkably similar to that I frequently experience with a great number of people from various countries on the African continent, both living within and without. Is all of the immediate above a series of conscious and calculated efforts, or simply a naïve and innocent cause and development of events? Which is which? What is behind this seemingly unnoticed situation that has captivated me and got me to be so interested and concerned about? Much more than often, I wonder whether being an African has to do with one's skin color, one's build, a particular ethnic feature, or the geographical location of the various countries on the African continent.

Everyone everywhere has an opinion or two about Africa and yet, only a small percentage of these people have any form of a relationship to this continent. The only tangible explanation that I have heard from people with proclaimed opinions is that their sources for forming these opinions usually do come from the media. So I have a huge interest in the very significant role played by the media. Famine, hunger, wars, an outbreak of diseases, political upheavals and instabilities, mismanagement, corruption, and all the other negatives associated with Africa.

It is not a secret that the media plays a very big role in the shaping of the societies commonly referred to as 'the developed countries'. I have often asked myself whether the media, especially in the 'developed countries' are aware of the magnitude of power that they yield. The media can make and break any establishment, be it political, social, cultural, or sports. Powerful politicians, sports personalities, entertainers, and musicians, all directly and indirectly benefit from the media apparatuses set up all over. But then again, why do the same media time and time again only bring negative news pictures from the African continent, especially parts inhabited by the dark-skinned section of the population?

All across the world, the images that are planted deep in our minds are usually those which are either directly manipulated or regulated in some form by those in authority. This I believe can either be by fair or foul means, however, do we even stop to think of how these images end up in our minds? This is by no means an effort of mine to proclaim that we do not have minds of our own to determine our fates, but my concern and interest in mentioning this is the effect it has on the perception of both the Africans and those from outside the African continent.

One of the goals I intend and hope to reach by writing this book is to someway, somehow, confront the whole world with this issue on the perception and belief, the misconceptions, the interpretations, the understanding that people have about Africa, her people, and the African continent as a whole.

My observations, interest and curiosity has nothing to do with accusing anyone of racism, no! There have been times when voicing out my concerns, or simply reacting to an already too familiar news bulletin or images on Africa, was met with counter reactions accusing me of insinuating the said situations to be racially motivated. This is far from the truth as it does sound surprising to some people when I state that there are many incidents involving other black people in and from other parts of the world (outside of the African continent) who have made expressions not that different to the widely presented negative views of Africa and for that matter, Africans of negro descent. Yes, some blacks from the US, England, the Caribbean, and elsewhere have expressed, directly or indirectly, their shame and discomfort in being connected either directly or indirectly to anything African, and on known occasions, even displaying their physical and emotional dissatisfaction as well. My observations and concerns are not to imply that the negative news and images of the African continent are racially motivated, but could they be?

As mentioned earlier, I hope with writing this book many observations I have made over so many years will either be shared by many or disputed; however, a light will be shed on the seemingly strange but thoroughly negative status of the African continent and her suffering people. In light of these observations, many questions might be answered and debated but one major goal I have is to create awareness of this mentioned situation which gets worse as the years go passing by.

On TV all across the 'developed countries', one cannot help but see numerous adverts day in and day out, appealing to people's compassion, sympathy and at times, even pity, to donate and help the 'poor African' people of their misery. Years ago, I was invited and participated in a TV studio debate program in the city of Odense, Denmark, on a topic along this same subject – something to do with the effect of the various donations made to the African countries by the non-profit, non-governmental and governmental organizations, and the mismanagement by all parties involved, and the consequences of their actions on the recipient African countries. This is a testament that in some way and somehow, my observations and concerns are not isolated.

As at the present, there is a huge increase in the number of all sorts of private organizations and private companies, all with the common message and goal of aiding Africa in every sector of her social setup: in the field of schooling and school materials for learning, food and clean water/water purification gadgets, electricity for lighting and medical operations, etc. This is as a matter of fact not new as much as I remember, but a daily occurrence from many years back, just that it's been intensified, with many more 'players' joining in lately. How come that the effect of all such massive actions over so many years has not made the situation and plight of the Africans better? In fact, there are clear signs and indications that many nations on the African continent's post-colonial era are worse off.

I hope for examining the reference and description of Africa by the international community when referring to the dark-skin populated regions will usually add the term – 'south of the Sahara', and what happened to the North African countries being referred to as Africans or the white settlers in Southern Africa and elsewhere on the continent? They should not have any problems or issues with being referred to as African countries. They are, after all, located on the main continent of Africa, same as would be referred to any European, South American countries located within the boundaries of the said continent.

This African continent is blessed with so much in terms of natural resources, gold, diamonds, rich vegetation, crude oil and gas, etc., which any nation on earth would proudly and willingly associate themselves with, right? Then how come the representation of Africa is always that of misery, poverty, degradation and negativity as a whole? Is there any reason? Common logic defies this very known and embraced status of sub-Saharan Africa and its people.

Pre-colonial and post-colonial African continent in the eyes of the international community cannot be clearly defined if one should ask them. The pictures and images of those innocent 'black Africans' commonly presented in literature, books, films and photographs by various entities both within and outside of the African continent as savages, war-mongers, animalistic, heathens, primitive, less-human, etc., has indeed barely changed. With all the post-colonial schooling and massive influence of the colonial powers on their colonies, there is very little to show for in the eyes of the international community, and I even think the result is catastrophic.

Indeed, Africa is a 'basket case', without whom the everyday worries and concerns of the international communities would be psychologically 'hanging' on them, but instead, it's ideal to have Africa bear all the negatives, which in turn makes those outside of Africa feel better. Why else? I frequently ask myself. The only times we hear or see images of Africa in the international news is to report on something negative, or rather patronizing to the African people, something we have heard and seen time and time again over a great number of years. Whosoever is presenting these negative news and images of Africa repeatedly over so many years and the situation of the Africans to whom these massive campaigns appealing to the compassion of the international community is not getting any better but rather getting worse, must be getting a 'pay off', a satisfaction, or a benefit from it. This makes me conclude and wonder as to whether there is any reason or cause to support my observation and subsequent conclusion.

Chapter 1
The African Continent

A very dear friend of mine in Denmark jokingly commented time and again on how they were introduced to the name "Africa" and what it meant during classes in their early school years. She would say in Danish, quote (I translate):

'Africa... a vast hot country...' unquote, just as dramatic as was told to them repeatedly by their then class teachers during class lessons apparently. I have sometimes struggled with my own sense of imagination and wrestled with the thought of picturing the images of these teachers illustrating by demonstrating with the movements of their arms and body. She will go on further to mimic the tone of voice with which these teachers will continue their teaching, quote:

'Africa, the country of giraffes, lions, monkeys, huge elephants, dangerous crocodiles', unquote:

A lady friend of mine casually mentioned to me during a conversation with her several years back about some of her travels, various eye-catching experiences and encounters. She made mention of a significant 1-day trip she took to visit Egypt whiles temporarily working in Israel. Geographically, Egypt borders Israel and has a common border crossing where people, goods and services regularly cross over. I enjoyed her story and found it fascinating enough to allow myself the opportunity of creating a picture of such a scenario, as often seen reflected in some photographs (both motion and still) as well as from movies and documentaries with scenes of busy border crossings and activities between two separate and independent communities, in my imagination of her story. In reacting to my own apparent involvement with her story, I uttered the statement:

'Wow, so you have visited Africa, that's nice!'

She reacted with a swift response in a way that took me aback.

'No, no, no, I did not visit Africa, I said I visited Egypt.'

'I heard you right, you have officially visited Africa,' I said.

She went on for some minutes to argue my point by stating uprightly that she had not been to Africa.

'Egypt is an African country, it is a country located on the African continent,' I said.

She then admitted to me in the most sincere way that she was not aware that Egypt was an African country and that Egyptians were indeed Africans.

I will attempt to describe the African continent as best as I can from the distant memory of my school years growing up in Ghana (located on the West coast of Africa), the country of my birth.

Africa is a continent with a large population, 2nd only to that of the Asian continent. The African continent consists of over 50 countries, independent of each other and commonly recognized and referred to (at least, to those of us who were raised in a country on the continent)

20

by its geographical divisions, i.e. North, Southern, East, West, Central, South Western, and not forgetting the big island nation of Madagascar in the very southeastern part of the continent, and the Cape Verde on the northwestern part. Some of the countries more commonly known in the northern part are Western Sahara, Morocco, Tunisia, Algeria, Libya, and Egypt. Directly below these North African countries lie the significant geographical landmark – The Tropic of Cancer – which borders a group of countries, notably: Mauritania (more to the Western coast), Mali, Niger, Chad, Sudan (stretching more to the east), lying between the North and the West African countries, occupying the West African coastal lines.

Notable countries located in the West are Senegal, The Gambia, Guinea-Bissau, Guinea, Sierra Leone, Liberia, Burkina Faso, Cote D´Ivoire, Ghana, Togo, Benin, Nigeria, Cameroon, Equatorial Guinea, and Gabon. To the east and central are The Central African Republic, The Democratic Republic of Congo, and the Republic of Congo. Moving to the Southern and South-Western part are Angola, Namibia, Zambia, Zimbabwe, Botswana, The Republic of South Africa, The Kingdom of Lesotho, The Kingdom of Swaziland, Mozambique, and The Republic of Madagascar to the south-eastern side in the Indian Ocean.

Moving up north to the center but still to the east are Malawi, Burundi, Tanzania, Rwanda, Kenya, Uganda, South; Sudan, Ethiopia, to the east, bordering Somalia, and up North, is Djibouti, Sudan, and Eritrea.

The year 2012 is almost over, and I have just seen a little part of a short film whiles writing this book and ironically, this short film tells of a very significant historic documentation of an event that relates directly to the African continent. According to this film, the African continent was divided amongst the various European countries and my understanding is that the present day borders between various African countries can be traced as far back to the year 1884, when the German Chancellor by the name of Otto von Bismarck gathered all the western powers, who already wielded much influence over their colonies in Africa, to discuss the sharing of the African continent amongst themselves. This meeting, which took place in Berlin, lasted four months and by the end of the meeting, those western diplomats had in principle decided the future of the African continent by satisfactorily and mutually agreeing to the introduction of various borders across the African continent, affecting thousands of locals and disrupting the local power base, forming a crucial factor in the later struggles of many African countries to gain their independence, plus the subsequent political turmoil that has disrupted the various African societies for many years up until the present day. People were divided against their will, creating primarily most of the borders existing to this present day.

The current status and picture even of the modern day African continent cannot be full and complete without the specific reference to the major role played by way of the massive influence of the foreign powers. Religious influence, political influence, cultural influence and all the other factors associated with a total influence in diverse ways on the African continent and its people.

I cannot continue without sharing some of the stories I have heard over the years regarding the origin of foreigners on the African continent, be it true or false. I start with that of the early Christian Missionaries who first arrived on the shores of the African continent.

The story is told that upon arrival to the shores of the African continent, in small boats attached to big ships which could ferry them to the mainland, these Missionaries presented to the local inhabitants the purpose of their travel to the African continent, which was to spread the word of God. In other words, their mission was to impart the Christian religious teachings to the locals with the intention of converting them into adopting the Christian knowledge and faith. Apparently, these missionaries were welcomed.

Knowing and judging by the characters of modern day African societies who willingly display hospitality, I believe those missionaries did really feel welcome. Anyway, the story goes on to tell us the eventual outcome of such an event, resulting in the beginning of the 'Slave Trade with Africans' on the African continent as we later came to learn about. I am sure many have seen the epic film version of the book – 'Shogun', the story of how some western explorers and travelers, notably the Dutch, in search of supposedly vast wealth in the Far East, ended up in faraway ancient Japanese Empire ruled by vicious and ruthless war Lords. The Dutch explorers, who had all along happily thought they were the first westerners to reach the shores of these rich lands, were bitterly disappointed to know that they had 'been beaten to the race' by Jesuit Missionaries from Portugal, who had many years earlier already had a footing in Japan and were indeed benefiting at great length from the lucrative trades they had established between themselves (on behalf of their countries) and their hosts.

The conclusion from this story is that for a great number of years in the pro-independence era of many of the African countries, many academicians and well-learned people on the African continent had a negative viewpoint and relationship to the Christian religious teachings. My point here is to present the similarities between the two above-mentioned events and try to draw conclusions from the legacy that these early foreign settlers left the African people. I have reserved a whole chapter on this subject later in the book, to try to debate on the pros and the cons, whiles trying to understand the effects on the African.

To come back on track, it's worth mentioning that a language is very important as an identifying tool to the entire existence of every human being, therefore, when on some occasions, I have been asked whether I speak African, and by this seemingly stupid but naïve question, I get the fact that many people outside of the African continent have completely no clue of what this continent and her people really are. But let me quickly point out that such questions usually come from rather smaller kids, whom for obvious reasons, have not been taught any meaningful thing about the continent of Africa, either in their schools or elsewhere.

French and English languages are predominantly spoken in the North African countries since there obviously are influences of their colonial past, however, these countries do speak their local languages as well. I really do not know whether they regard the languages imposed on them by the colonial rulers as their official languages, as it's the case with many of the southern dark-skin dominated countries.

French and English languages are considered the official languages of most of the countries in the South, and rightfully so, dominate both identities and existence of the communities. Ghana, my country of birth and located on the West Africa coastline, has English as the official language due to its colonial past where the British were the last colonial rulers and prior to achieving her independence in 1957. To the east of Ghana lies Togo and to her west is Cote D'Ivoire. Bordering Ghana directly to the North is Burkina Faso, and these three independent countries bordering Ghana all have French as their official language. It is interesting to know that the various community settlers on both sides in these border areas actually do have family relations with the other. I know personally of a community on the border separating Ghana from Togo where one can experience exact similarities in the way the communities on both sides of the border function. Most are related by way of family, the community rules, language, norms, identities, and yet divided by the common border introduced by the political powers far away, and officially enforced by the introduction of these official languages – English and French.

It strikes a serious blow to me when I think about the magnitude of dilemma those of us who truly care are faced with. Come to think for the sake of a little brain game, the make-up and structure of the African continent, from the north to the south, and east to west. That can be a serious challenge since, in my own little attempt to summons a clear view summary of the makeup of the African continent, I get confused. There are over fifty independent sovereign countries, all having an official language representing them internationally.

If we take Ghana, for example, the official language representing them is English. Besides this official language are several tribal languages.

Chapter 2
The Image of the African Continent

The time is 16:53 this Thursday afternoon. It has been dark, gray, wet and cold for the most part of the day on this official winter season here in Copenhagen, Denmark. I am back in my seat after some minutes of staring out the window with a cup of warm tea in my hand, whiles doing some stretches from the strain of long sitting periods.

The constant edge in me to follow the news prompts me to turn on the TV and with the help of the remote control, scramble leisurely, searching for a preferable news channel. I come across a number of uninteresting channels but notice 3 channels that catch my attention and though I am inclined to keep pressing the buttons on the remote control in continuing my search, I stop on a channel which is showing an advertisement from a known Danish-based international organization appealing to viewers to notice the situation of a young black girl, apparently an "African" girl, walking away in distress. I have seen this advertisement so many times in the past couple months so out of irritation, I quickly press to another one of the 3 previous channels that I had skipped a few seconds earlier.

This channel irritates me even more and I act even more swiftly to change to the 3rd channel in mind. I had quickly noticed a similar advert from another established and known Danish international organization, with a similar message as the one earlier, except that this message is, in my opinion, an attempt to be explicit and humble. But I have as well seen this advert along half a dozen others, with either the same or similar messages.

The third channel immediately catches my attention as there was a debate between 2 individuals, each representing a political wing or interest. The debate was about poverty and was taking place in a radio studio. I had noticed that one of the Danish Radio and TV stations had earmarked the entire week to discuss poverty.

"*Poverty*"! I thought to myself, is a word I have heard so often, however, under a completely different reference. I sat comfortably in my chair to follow this debate which turned out to be about whether poverty existed in Denmark or not.

'I have debated this in my head many times,' I had said to myself, but of course, not in the same context as to having to do with Denmark. No! I just could hear and feel a similar concern and anxiety. The primary observation in this very interesting debate for me was the conclusion as to the ultimate result with regards to what the perception of being poor can be for those who feel poor and those who see others as poor.

The mention of my reaction to the 2 TV channels that were showing their apparent massive efforts in appealing to the general public for donations and other forms of contribution to the seemingly permanent state of the African continent simply irritates me.

'Why react that way, is it not so?' Some will ask. Well, it is, I guess. How else can I be defensive of my irritable position when I rather should be grateful that others are making efforts to help the very terrible situation in Africa, right? Well, my answer is no!

I do not believe I am the only one in the entire universe who wonders why there seems to be no end to this constant appeal to help the "Africans". Is the situation of the "Africans" ever going to change, or it's a permanent situation we must accept and learn to live with? I cannot! It makes no sense to me. Firstly, there are millions of questions need put and be answered.

There seem to be a 'thing' with the areas usually inhabited by the dark-skinned population that is frequently in the news on whose behalf massive aid is needed and appealed for. Time and time again, we hear of, and witness by way of photos or TV, either Ethiopia, Somalia, Eritrea, or Kenya needing massive aid in diverse forms, often due to some type of natural disorder, with devastating consequences for the inhabitants and the list goes on. Other times, we hear of the whole of West Africa, or another region plagued by famine due again to some unforeseen form of natural mishap.

If I was to ask people randomly anywhere about what comes to mind when they hear the name "Africa", I am sure most will answer in pure innocence, along the following: poverty, hunger, famine, diseases, degradation, incompetence, hopelessness, lack of self-help, inadequacies, dull, unintelligent, and all the various negative attributes of a human being.

I saw an advert on TV last PM. The Christmas month of December is in its infancy and the atmosphere is as it

29

always is, oozing with the usual Christmas spirit being felt in the air and all around. This ad, as expected, is just one of the many from the dozens of organizations who, I am sure, have good intentions to reach out and help the needy in Africa, as they very comfortably like to present it as. It is an ad involving a couple of young guys from the hip-hop culture, presumably in Denmark. These hip-hop guys (giving the scenery in the film) are on the local scene I guess and joined by a number of the local kids, whiles a hip-pop song is being played to the movements of all the actors. As expected, there are some mud-built huts in the background, symbolizing the atmosphere of 'the Africa' as we have come to know, and the local boys of different sizes but shirtless, making movements identical to that we know of the established hip-pop culture – 'doing the dance-move expressions with attitude'.

The name of this Danish organization is 'Boernefonden', directly translating into English as: 'The Children's Fund'. I made a telephone call to them, just as I had done some other times in the past and as I had expected, I was engaged in a short dialog with a lady representative from their advert and marketing department whom the receptionist had rightfully connected my call to, for being the responsible person to answer any questions I might have in that regard. Notwithstanding my expectation of not making any meaningful impact with my call, as has been the case in the past, with all the other several calls and queries I have made to similar organizations in the past. I was determined to get 'a voice' through to them. There were several questions and concerns that I tried putting through. Questions and concerns that are elaborated in different bits and forms in its full entirety in this book, but it felt like I so often do, 'hit a wall'.

'It is Africa and they need help,' many would think and react, therefore, a majority of people automatically draw to such conclusions and thereby creating an instance of status quo.

I have often wondered, in consideration of the extent to which money and finance has played and still plays a role even more so today than ever, in whose interest the stereotype images often displayed of "Africa and Africans" are maintained and continuously propagated to the international community serves, often without regard for the long-term effect of the innocent people from the African continent?

The cynicism in all of this is that as much as it is apparent of the aspiration and goal of the 'players' in concentrating on the efforts to get as many donors, Aid and assistance, the image created out there in the international community, be it through the media or otherwise, seems to be a vital key. This has, in my opinion, created an atmosphere displaying the intent and goal through the numerous projects worldwide by shareholders and interest organizations and, in some cases, exposing conflicting agendas.

It seems to be very important (for some reason) for some in the international community to manipulate with the very same negative image that they have helped create.

A continent made up of so many different communities and populated by over 1 billion people with a vast diversity; cultural, ethnic, religious and more, plus, with so much wealth and riches, can be presented in the most demeaning and abominable ways, just to serve a purpose. The purpose is, of course, arguable to many, but there is no doubt in the minds of those who care to know, that it serves the agendas of 'someone somewhere'.

The image of sub-Sahara African societies and its dark-skin population is unquestionably a means to self-glorification for some and financial gains for others because the ratio regarding the population of "Africans" and the 'few' who supposedly benefit, does not fit, in relation to the messages and information that precede the numerous campaigns for the all-important Aid and Economic Assistance, making me question why nothing seems to change but rather, the efforts to keep the negative image is intensified.

Who has not, in one form or the other, seen the images of "Africa and Africans" in compromising situations sometimes unbefitting that of human beings? Who has at a point in time or the other, not seen the infamous 'poor, malnourished and skinny-looking African children with flies all over their faces'? There might be some who have 'had enough', and others who might be immune to these images of the dark-skin people in sub-Sahara African societies, but it apparently makes no difference to those who manipulate with and distort the reality.

Chapter 3
Prejudice

I love sports in general, mostly due to my background in being very active in almost all sporting activities when I was younger, but notably in football, also known as soccer. The passion for football lives and thrives very well in me, but more as an enthusiastic fan. All types of sports do generate an immense interest in me, so much that I usually see myself following both live games and reports, either via TV or other forms of media.

I have so often wondered why the comments, information and live commentaries on sporting events involving either a participant or a team from a 'black African' country are so one-sided, negative, filled with a lot of prejudice, unfair judgment and ignorant conclusions.

Am I the only one who has noticed on several occasions where certain remarks are uttered to either describe an incident or make reference to these 'black Africans' involved in the actions in question?

Do not get me wrong, the preference to use the term 'black' in describing the Africans that I am referring to here is to try as much as I can to not generalize, whiles emphasizing the point that in no way am I directly accusing anyone of being a racist, though there can be some tendencies since we are all human. I would very much like to support this position I have taken by citing a very vivid example that some friends of mine experienced several years back.

'Casanova' was a nightclub in the center of Copenhagen and frequented by lots of non-ethnic Danes but rather immigrants from other parts of the world who, for one reason or the other, preferred to rather spend time in this club. There were mostly people of different race, color, and stature other than ethnic Danes, who patronized 'Club Casanova'. Those were good times when remembering the 'Brothers' (inter-black men referencing each) from 'The States' who were stationed at some US military bases in Northern Germany and surroundings, visiting the club at weekends. This club did also attract quite a number of young ethnic Danish women, probably due to the expected atmosphere, which was without a doubt very different from that of the other Danish nightclubs. As would be expected, there was some competition between some of the men to 'win' the ladies and one repeated incident witnessed, as well as personal encounters with others, is that the 'Brothers' from 'The States' were aggressively using a method of painting the credentials of the 'Brothers' from Africa. Note, this is an incident involving 2 parties, both of black skin origin.

'He is from Africa, he is from Africa,' a phrase the US 'Brothers' kept hammering into the minds of these ladies in the club to convince them not to fall for any offensive attempts by the 'African brothers' to win them over but rather, settle for them – the US 'Brothers'.

Being prejudicial, I guess, is a character we all have in one form or the other but my personal observation has indicated so often to me, and continues to this day, is in the field of Sports. I personally find it appalling to listen to the so-called experts and commentators on various sporting events involving Africans.

By this, I am referring specifically to participants of these sporting events who are of dark-skin descent. The remarks and comments which are continuously made directly impacts my observation and leads to my conclusion, be it right or wrong.

If you are a regular follower of soccer/football games, you definitely might have heard of this expression: 'An African tackle'. This is a direct reference, presumably to a particularly hard and rough tackle by one player on the opposing player and for some mysterious reason (at least to me), it is accepted and even embraced in my circles even as at the present. Being a very enthusiastic soccer/football lover, I have witnessed many games across the globe, both live and via TV transmission, and I am yet to see how this unfair perception is so. It just beats my sense of understanding that no one has protested to such a perception when day in and day out, there are several of similar and even worse tackles in the highly professional games around the world.

Still on the subject of football/soccer, the biannual tournament to find the best football/soccer nation on the African continent, known as the 'African Cup of Nations' is about to begin and to some of us based in Europe, we get to see it televised live on the sports TV channels known as – Eurosport. This coming edition is a little odd because for technical reasons explained by the governing bodies, it is being held a year after the last so as to avoid this big international tournament being staged in an even year so as to avoid an eventual clash with the FIFA arranged World Championship, which is held every four years in an even year, apparently. It is so clear when following these games how much of the time these experts and commentators use in talking about everything strange, wrong, and superstitious about "Africa and Africans" and so little is said about the game itself that they are commenting on. This same pattern is repeated each and every time this tournament is being televised as if nothing has been learnt in the previous televised games.

During the tournament itself, the Eurosport channels do have an arrangement whereby viewers can send in a text message with comments or questions regarding the particular game that is being televised for minimum charges, and it never ceases to amaze me as to how prejudicial the 'outside world' is, on the African continent and its people. As mentioned above, it's been quite some years now since these African football championship games have been beamed live onto the TV screens across Europe and elsewhere (at least 16 years), yet I have observed the same or similar comments and questions being presented, time and time again. The question I am left with is whether anyone makes any effort to find out at least some of the facts and fiction about and connected to this continent?

How often do we hear the expression – 'world tour' (in connection with some form of entertainment, music concert, sporting event, educational event, etc.) where the African continent is included?

I will bet anyone to disagree with me when I conclude that the name "Africa" is synonymous with everything 'negative' and nothing good to write home about.

I have had the gracious opportunity of being engaged in several diplomatic missions in rendering different services on their behalf, and some of these experiences were with diplomatic missions of some African countries. Uganda, Ghana, Lesotho, and Swaziland are some of the embassies I have worked for. The statuses of the missions and the diplomats are like all other diplomatic representations of other countries. The embassy buildings, official motor vehicles, and properties are all on a level with those of other countries and do sometimes even surpasses those of others, especially the developed countries and the known rich ones as well. The daily engagements were no different than it is with duties connected with the functions of a diplomatic representation across the globe.

On one of the duties as a chauffeur for the diplomatic mission of the Kingdom of Swaziland (an independent country enclosed by the Republic of South Africa) in a European country capital, I was leading a group of diplomatic officers on an errand to one of the popular furniture shops in the city to purchase a wide selection of furniture to furnish the homes of majority of the diplomats. It was a total of 5 homes altogether and expected to be an expensive purchase. A cashier's check, a huge sum of money had been written out for the eventual payment to the furniture shop from where the purchase would take place. I had no doubt in my mind whatsoever that the check amount was more than twice the daily sales of this furniture shop we were to deal with.

As expected, the diplomats in our party were all in the official suit and tie and so was I. In entering this popular furniture shop, we proceeded to the 'customer service' desk to consult and ask for assistance. Part of my duties was to lead in the verbal communication due to my knowledge in the use of the language spoken in this particular European country, however, I had decided on purpose not to start the verbal conversation due to my past experiences with the many white people from this European country, just to see their reaction. So I started by speaking in English, which was quickly joined in by my diplomat companions.

In the midst of our discussions with the furniture shop representative relating to the pros and cons of our choices, I heard a loud comment in the local language coming from the customer desk. A female employee, amongst her colleagues from the customer desk, apparently found it necessary to comment on how useless it is for them (the furniture shop) to use time on us because we were not capable of purchasing what we had indicated we would.

'Do not use time on them, they are only wasting our time and are not capable of paying for all that furniture they are showing interest in, what do you expect from Africans?' She said.

What she apparently was not aware of was that I understood their language and therefore reacted by asking their staff present of what her comment was about. I, of course, narrated the lady's comment to my accompanying diplomats in English, who in turn demanded an explanation from the management of the furniture shop for such disrespect shown them.

A man and a woman from their management team approached us trying to explain to us, stating that their colleague from the customer service's comment had been misunderstood by us and that they apologize for that misunderstanding. Out of the anger and frustration, one of the diplomats took out the prepared check (which had the name of the furniture shop inscribed on it) and displayed it to the furniture shop management team, making them aware of the large amount on the check which was meant to be a payment to the furniture shop for what would have been purchased.

We indicated shortly after our intention to desist from our intended purchase of furniture from their shop and were boycotting their shop, and any future dealings with them.

As expected, the management team put in a lot of effort to dissuade us from leaving and boycotting them as we had threatened, and came in with many offers to help change our minds and rescind our decision.

Prejudice towards dark-skin communities on the African continent south of the Sahara is so mind-blowing.

As mentioned in other parts of this book, as the call for their leaders to react to the refugee crisis in Europe increased and people's worries intensified, the government leaders of the European countries needed to show some 'punching power' and take immediate firm action. Who else is better to be at the receiving end of the wrath of Europe, represented by their leaders, than "Africans"? Why would any European want to have the "Africans" in their midst? 'They are primitive, uncultured, illiterate, uncivilized, disease-infested, lazy and inferior people and do not belong amongst Europeans;' I am sure might be the conclusion of many, and the underlining factor for the actions of the European leaders. An urgent top meeting in Malta was arranged between the European Union leaders and the African Union leaders, involving some financial settlement for the African leaders to take back their citizens. Since this action, the European Union leaders are yet to fully implement other decisions to send back other refugee and migrants from other countries. In summarizing the efforts being made in desperation, the European Union leaders entered into an agreement with Turkey to stop the use of their territories as starting points of the illegal travels into Greece and other European countries; with Turkey being the beneficiary of a substantial financial payment package.

I still have in my possession a newspaper article that I cut out because of the effect the content had on me. A Danish powerful Trade Union was informing the public of their decision to pull out their investments from Africa and invest in Southeast Asia instead due to the fact that 'the Africans' were not productive enough to their liking.

Some years earlier, an extensive documentary was made on the state of Africa and Africans, relating to social growth. The producers of this documentary received positive reviews and even verbal endorsements from the Danish business and political elite. It was such an awkward presentation in which the focus of what was positive and negative was primarily via expatriate business people operating in but a few chosen African countries in the eastern and southern part of the continent. The conclusions were to demonstrate through various ways on the negatives of the said communities; slow thinkers, their inability to quickly learn and catch up on the training given them, them being lazy and unreliable and all the negative narratives.

After seeing that documentary, I was left with a bitter taste in my mouth as to the purpose of such a documentary. There were interviews made with both expatriate and local owners of companies that employed the locals. Factories, construction, transport, agriculture and other production lines had lots of locals in employment. In the interviews, all emphasis was on the negative impact the local employees had on the entire development of the society, according to the employers. The conclusion in this documentary film is the effort of the filmmakers to present the local; the "African", as being non-productive and a nonentity.

In the services for a diplomatic mission to an African country, I went to the international airport in the company of a couple of their diplomats to pick up the diplomatic bag which is monthly flown in from their Ministry of Foreign Affairs back in their home country. This duty consists of a variety of formalities involving visiting different departments at the cargo section of the national air carrier and to fulfill an official requirement of documentation in order to get the diplomatic bag released to us. In the midst of the bureaucratic procedure arose a misunderstanding between us and the different departments, making it cumbersome to locate the diplomatic bag. All the while, we were communicating with the airline staff in English, there were verbal

41

remarks made supposedly due to the frustration of the situation by some of their staff in their local language.

In our reactions to the strange puzzle of where the diplomatic bag could be, a hectic debate ensued between our party and theirs. In this ensuing heated debate, one of the staff members accused our party of lying about not having taken over the diplomatic bag. The staff member went on to mention in her attempt to justify her accusation, how she had lived in Africa for a while back and her experiencing the constant lying on the part of the Africans. She went on further to emphasize in her accusation on how lying was very normal to Africans, and that it was deeply planted in their culture. Her point was that lying was part of the culture of Africans; therefore, our continuous position of awaiting the diplomatic bag to be given to us was nothing but a charade from our side. This accusation infuriated my diplomatic companions, who made an official complaint to the management of the airline. The diplomatic bag was traced to another area of the cargo section, due apparently to a malfunction of their computing system that expedites the receipt and registration of all special cargo into the country via the international airport.

My overriding observation of the widespread prejudicial perception and treatment of sub-Saharan Africa and its citizens are undeniably strongly connected in a big part, to ignorance, and whereas it might seem normal to many, I find it absurd, even more, when it is officially displayed on national TV by people in positions who are supposed to know better.

At the end of an international conference on global climate in a European country Capital and participated by top world leaders, governments and NGOs, an incident was captured on a film, documenting the entirety of this important global event. With my knowledge of duties required of diplomatic missions accredited abroad, I had imagined the vigorous demand that will come to bear on the host government, especially on their Ministry of Foreign Affairs, who has a great deal of responsibility regarding the organization of such global conferences. Without having to go into details as to some of the unwelcoming experiences by a few delegates representing some sub-Sahara African countries that I got to know of, a clear display of prejudice was glaringly recorded, which I thought was unfortunate. In the seemingly chaotic supervision of the departure from the airport of the many foreign dignitaries who had participated in this global conference, a woman representing either the airline or the protocol department of the host country's Foreign Ministry was struggling in coordinating her duties. In one of the airport departure lounges, there was a discussion between the airport personnel led by this woman and some delegates representing a country in sub-Saharan Africa, relating to an apparent lapse in the coordination of their luggage and their departure time. During this discussion, the film crew who had been filming all along asked the lady what the apparent misunderstanding was all about and she responded directly into the camera on how she was tired of the lack of understanding from the group she was attending to.

'Their culture is an impediment to their understanding and makes me frustrated,' she said.

'It takes too much energy to get them organized, unlike the others we assist daily and all that is because of their culture,' she added.

I saw a television documentary a few days ago about the wealthiest people in the world, their lifestyles, their relationships to the outside world and how the outside world views them. In relating to this program, I had followed another TV documentary on the wealthy and the rich and their influence in what they referred to as the emerging societies, amongst which were countries like Vietnam and India named. Wealth and riches, without any doubt, influences the view and perception of all societies around the world, be it big or small, and I dare say much more than we care to admit.

The continuous unfair treatment given to sub-Saharan Africa can be summed to the simple notion and perception that the societies there are poor, very poor in the physical sense.

Dark-skin people in and from sub-Saharan Africa are openly subjected to discrimination, hatred and racism of the worse kind just because they are seen and perceived as physically poor. What I think is grotesque about this is the simple fact that the status of Africa being poor, apart from the effects of natural disasters, wars, famine, etc. is that there are many other communities around the world who have equally poor conditions. Communities in Asia, South America, even places in Europe and North America, without them, subjected to hatred, racism and the likes just because they are poor.

In continuing with the aforementioned subject of the TV documentary about the wealthy and rich people in emerging societies, I was struggling with understanding

44

the importance of the apparent respect and admiration derived from the positions of the display of wealth riches.

'But why then is it not so with communities in sub-Saharan Africa?' I ask myself.

'If showing riches and wealth in abundance can be a prerequisite for outright respect, recognition and admiration, then the various communities in sub-Saharan Africa would not have to be subjected to the all-too-familiar perception and negative treatment from the international community,' I would add.

Not that it should really matter in terms of the perspective of the many disadvantaged in sub-Sahara African communities, but in realizing how important it is for the perception which carries a lot of weight for how a society or community is viewed and perceived, then I find it necessary to bring to the awareness of the international community of similar wealth and riches in many sub-Sahara African communities.

In this documentary, I heard a female person make mention of how the rich and the wealthy influenced a particular city in India. She mentioned how the city beamed with wealth and riches, which could be seen as soon as one comes into the city. In distant relation to the same subject, there was the mention of Vietnam and how rapid development, despite the very difficult times after the Vietnam War, has given positive results and created a society with many emerging wealthy and rich people. This is apparently news worth presenting to the international community, presumably because it is a known fact that money, wealth and riches do create prestige in every society, which in turn commands some level of respect. Going by this simple fact, "Africa", as it is commonly referred to as, but more in reference to the dark-skin people in the sub-Saharan region of the African continent, should also command some respect no matter the volume.

It is important for me to stress on this subject again, that there is also a level of wealth and riches in many of the sub-Sahara African communities similar, equaled and even surpassing that of those societies, some of which are mentioned in here, that the international community chooses to embrace and admire. If wealth and riches are underlining factors in determining the level of respect people and societies deserve, then it is right to mention that "Africa" does not deserve the negative treatments around the world. Just because the international community, in their twisted-minded agenda to hold a people hostage and deny them the recognition to be valued and respected, chooses to rather present every negative and distorted news and images and ignore what they themselves admire and respect of others, should not mean that the people and communities in sub-Saharan Africa should continuously be looked down on and considered a 'basket case'. It surprises me that this has gone on for so long and has left a very serious negative print in the heads of many people, which in turn dictates, directly and indirectly, the way dark-skin people from sub-Saharan African are treated around the world.

Help and assistance, sympathy, kindness, compassion in diverse ways to the poor, weak, and the needy, from the strong, the rich, the privileged, are distinct basic qualities of being human but it is paradoxical in many ways to me because one (definitely, I) would think that having all indications of poverty, and in the case of

"Africa", extreme poverty for that matter being presented day in and out, would trigger the goodness in people in assisting and helping but it is rather the opposite. Being presented rich and wealthy as compared to being poor and needy has a significant impact in the way one is perceived by the international community. In the case of "Africa" – dark-skin people and communities in sub-Saharan Africa – this image is a serious contributing factor to how they are treated around the world. The images planted in the minds of people around the world seems to be the only reference by which sub-Saharan African communities are viewed and treated, which is often without respect, dignity, inhuman, and looked down on.

In my several attempts to create a debate on this issue, I have often engaged some people in seeking their opinions and in one of such discussions in a European city with a male citizen of that country, I showed a photo typical of the ones known from disaster situations connected with the continent of Africa, especially in the sub-Saharan region. This photo was of a woman, presumably the mother in a kneeling posture over a toddler that could be her child. Both the woman and the child were malnourished beyond recognition of being human. They were both 'eaten down to the bone', and very difficult to comprehend how any human being could disintegrate to nothing short of skin and bones.

His reaction was that of calmness and with a sigh, his response was that which is well known to some of us who have for a long time cared to know. His belief and honest opinion, which could not be far from the truth, was that many people from the international community had become immune to such images and therefore, do not get affected.

Chapter 4
The Media

Our everyday living is directly influenced by the role played by the media and even more so than we are willing to confront. This is a fact, whether we like to confront it or not. I could allow myself the privilege of a spot in the limelight by certain possible controversies deriving from my mere mention and focus on this subject, or need I do so?

The Eiffel Tower symbolizes Paris, the city of romance, and the French Republic. The Statue of Liberty, the Empire State Building, the skylines of New York, Miami, and Chicago are all symbols of wealth, power, and progress of the United States of America as well as the western world. I remember the early days when most of us were enticed by the intro of the 'soap series – Dallas,', featuring the infamous 'JR', the accompanying signature tune and the glamor of even the 'country' life that preceded each episode. It was just another symbolic form, enforcing what the life in the US is, supposedly.

I just saw a documentary program about the art of dancing. Time and time again, I heard the mention of the Tango dance, directly connecting the name – Argentina. Of course, Tango is a dance originating from Argentina and practiced around the world. The mention of Brazil easily rings a bell in the ears of many around the world for her famous Copacabana beach, the Rio Carnival, and best of all, football or soccer. The list of various independent societies around the world and the positive meanings of the symbols attached to their names can go on and on.

Africa! Africa! Africa! What comes to mind by the mere mention of Africa? Ironically, I would glaringly bet on the fact that a hundred percent of all mankind on this earth, including those making up the population on the African continent, will without giving it much thought, conclude unanimously all the 'befitting' adjectives qualifying the images and pictures in our heads.

Malnourished children crying helplessly, covered in 'coats of utter desperation', and often displays of hopelessness. This is indeed some of the repeated images soundly implanted involuntarily in our heads, but by whom?

Both adults and kids usually topless and without 'proper' footwear, in a seemingly very hot, dry and barren landscape in the background, following a flock and herd of some domestic animals, be it cattle or sheep, looking hungry and bewildered. A group of primitive black men and women gathered around a tree or a bonfire singing or expressively uttering some noises known only to them. The most recognizable image of them all: that of skinny-lean-bony men, women, and especially children with desperate looks on their faces, in over-crowded areas, seemingly refugee camps, having fled some sort of famine, wars, or a tribal conflict. Is the picture I am attempting to paint of "Africa and Africans" in your heads close to that you are so familiar with?

Unless I am exaggerating, the few times news on Africa appears in the news media, is in direct connection with something bad, like famine, hunger, destitution, diseases, etc. and this has become a cultural thing with the international media which keeps being repeated time and time again. In reacting to my frequent frustrations over the constant presentation of this one-sided news on Africa, I have often made several attempts for direct contacts to the sources of such news reporting, often unsuccessful. Why, I ask, is it that all we hear and know about Africa is that of misery, hopelessness, despair, destitution, poverty, and everything negative? I have often heard and read about the "Africans" being primitive.

I would say in defense of a lot of journalists that, just like many others around the world, the lack of interest to know, plus a great dose of ignorance is, without a doubt, the major reason for their continuous misrepresentation of the African continent and its citizens south of the Sahara.

The actions of the international media in relation to the picture and images of the people from the various communities in sub-Saharan Africa is in my opinion, one of the true injustices against humanity because they usually are one-sided. I would think the duties of the media are amongst others, to look out for the positive interest of the public and help fight expose the negative forces and activities detrimental to the society. In most cases, the media represents an arm of the government of the society in building a reputation of doing good, something like a watchdog, uncovering different forms of wrong-doings, exposing the dark side of public officials and the dirt in society. In relation to their job, it is expected of the dedicated and professional media people to do their homework very well in order to be credible with the public. How come such high standards are not applied when doing work on sub-Saharan Africa?

In these early days of the year 2016, I am extremely negatively surprised at the role played by the international media towards sub-Saharan Africa and its people. I would think that with time and the developments around the world, especially in the area of Information Technology, the media would tackle global subjects with a neutral sense and for the benefit of all. This is in the least, with special reference to the media with global interest, interest for all people in this world. From the constant discriminatory attitude of the international media, one would think that they have an agenda in their actions, or do they?

It is disheartening to me when I see the wide coverage on TV or in other forms of media news coverage on people from other places facing some prolonged or stagnant conditions in after-disaster periods, seemingly to the exclusion of people from sub-Saharan Africa. This is in no way an attempt to diminish or disparage the seriousness and importance of people around the world who have had to experience such ordeals, be it by nature or man-made, but to question the reason behind the seemingly deliberate actions on the side of the international media relating to sub-Saharan Africa and its people who have, unfortunately, been put in similar situations. I am tempted to question the actions of the international media in their apparent double-standard and discriminatory behaviors towards sub-Saharan Africa and its people.

The best arguments that I have been faced with in the times I have requested for the explanation to why the media seemingly have such double-standards is that of the lack of better knowledge, but one would otherwise think it's both their moral and ethical responsibility to get the knowledge and right information.

As I have pointed out in other parts of this book, why should the refugee and migrant crisis facing Europe in the years 2015 and 2016 overshadow the equally appalling situation in East Africa and other parts of sub-Saharan Africa? Why is it that the international media exhibits a lack of interest in covering the long-standing refugee and migrant crisis, wars and natural disaster situations affecting the numerous sub-Sahara African communities?

Often, it takes a very extensive intervention, usually from known people – international celebrities– or massive pressure forcing the international media into action. The consequences, as we know, are often with catastrophic consequences for the people.

Are the lives of the people from the communities in sub-Saharan Africa of no relevance? I often ask myself.

For as long as I can remember, information (be it right or wrong) relating to the sub-Sahara African region and its people through the media has been dominated by the 'negatives'. The international media seems to be on a campaign of negative presentation when relating to sub-Saharan Africa. History tells us of the methods used during slavery and colonial times on the African continent, and for some reason, the international media has continued in the distortion of information relating to the communities in sub-Saharan Africa, directly enforcing the negative image, myths, prejudices, xenophobia, and all the negative narratives.

More than 98% of what is known of the communities from sub-Saharan Africa, especially the world outside of the African continent and even within the African continent as well, is via the international media, signifying their immense influence on the general perception the world has in sub-Saharan Africa and its people.

Schools in Western Europe, Eastern Europe, Asia, Australasia, North America, South America, North Africa, and even some parts of expatriate-dominated sub-Saharan Africa have a distorted presentation of what the African continent is, thus, a great majority of people, both adults and young, know no other information and end up continuing with this huge portion of ignorance relating to sub-Saharan Africa.

The underlining reason for one human to assume the right to possess and dominate another must be the twisted perception of being more of a human than the other, which in my debatable conclusion, can be compared to the way sub-Saharan Africa and its citizens are treated by the international community whose actions can only be due to the images and pictures presented to them via the international media.

In symbolizing places around the world; the Eiffel Tower for Paris, the London Bridge, the Big Ben and the British Queen's palace guards for London, the White House, and the New York, Chicago, or other US city skylines, the Red Square for Russia, the Great Wall of China and the Sydney Opera House for Australia, the international media are as yet to be "gracious" to sub-Sahara African countries. Instead, they have without opposition, chosen to symbolize one significant country in North Africa which is Egypt, by the images of the Pyramids and the rest sub-Sahara African countries by using the pictures of elephants, zebras, antelopes, lions, etc. in their wild natural surroundings.

It is important to add that such presentation of Africa as described immediately above must be considered as being the positive presentation to the international community or alternatively, the images of degradation, poverty, misery, famine, malnourished people and animals, animal carcasses, barren and dry landscape, very young and old men keeping watch over grazing livestock, would be the usual acceptable presentation, so symbolic of what Africa is.

In the true sense of the meaning of exploitation, I would not hesitate to claim that the role of the international media could not have served as a better platform from where the exploiters could do what they do best; the aid organizations, dictators and corrupt leaders on the African continent, foreign companies, to name a few.

In the early 1980s when the outbreak of the deadly HIV virus causing the AIDS disease was everyday news, it was no surprise that the international media was presenting the eventual source as being in Africa. As has always been, the ignorance of the masses in relation to the African continent is constantly fed by the international media, without attempts to question or debunk their conclusions. Speculations and guesswork relating to the original source of the HIV virus have become a common topic of discussion in the public forum and before long, it had become an acceptable conclusion that the virus originates from Africa. The reason for this acceptable perception is that the HIV virus had apparently crossed from primates to humans due to the simple fact that Africans ate monkeys as part of their diets.

I remember so well an informative TV program I saw in Denmark during those tense times in which a woman, who had apparently been infected with the virus, gave the account of the circumstances of how she came into contact with the virus. She told the studio audience of how she had traveled to Africa, and had sexual intercourse with a local man who was definitely her source for being infected with the HIV virus.

It's the middle of the 80s. Campaigns and information to combat the AIDS epidemic has intensified and unsurprisingly, a newspaper article appears in one of the leading newspapers, sending out a message supposedly from a leading medical Doctor from one of the leading hospitals, directly warning Danish women not to engage in any sexual act with Africans.

Days after this article appearing in the newspapers, there was a very strong reaction from a number of diplomatic missions of the majority of African countries accredited to Denmark. I happened to be physically present in the offices of a particular embassy whose ambassador had been the leader of the embassies of the various African countries, protesting against this article in the newspaper. The African countries' embassies were obviously reacting to what they considered as a collective insult in the too often generalization by the media and the public as a whole. I got to know that the ambassador had summoned his colleagues from the other embassies of the African countries and sent an official strong protest through the Danish Ministry of Foreign Affairs.

The goal of the ambassadors in sending this protest was to show their dissatisfaction with the media and the general public for the newspaper article unfairly generalizing and disrespecting the whole people from one continent; the sub-Saharan region. To achieve this goal, the ambassadors had demanded, through the Danish Ministry of Foreign Affairs, the newspaper company to publish another article apologizing to the entire African continent, as well as withdrawing the earlier article.

Several days went by without seeing any such article of apologies appearing in the same newspaper so the embassies contacted the protocol department of the Danish Foreign Ministry to follow up on their earlier action and request for an apology and withdrawal of the article. The response from the Danish Ministry of Foreign Affairs was that the newspaper company had confirmed that they had rendered an apology in an earlier edition of the newspaper publication. A search was undertaken by the embassies and shortly after did, in fact, confirm the claim that had been made by the newspaper company and such article was located in an earlier publication. The odd feeling this action left the embassies as well as some of us concerned onlookers, was that this article was so tiny in print and appeared on a page reserved for other non-political and non-current affairs subjects. To sum it all up, this small and almost insignificant article of apology from the newspaper company was to simply put, ineffective; the damage was already done. Though an official apology had been given by this news media, this deliberate action on their part was not effective enough to counteract the damage already caused by the earlier big article which had been front-page news.

The efforts of the international media are undeniably effective in separating the African countries north of the Sahara from the rest, which is made evident by people's ability to refer to them by their real names; Egypt, Tunisia, Morocco, Libya, instead of "Africa". These North-African countries were very successful in the tourism business and attracted massive holiday makers and tourists, which in turn generated lots of foreign capital for them. It is no secret that the image and pictures representing these countries matched that of luxury, vacationing, and tourism. This is a factor which has contributed immensely to the positive image connected to these countries, making it impossible to fall under the generalizing game played by the international media. People do know what the countries in North-Africa are by name and not just by a collective term or reference. It is fair to say that this description is a contributing factor to why the individual countries have a positive image and have succeeded in not being included in the usual collective term: "Africa", which we all know is directly connected with negativity.

Not that it should really matter but I am sure many would agree with me that if pictures depicting modern architecture, high-rise buildings, multi-carriage streets and highways, smiling children in presentable school uniforms, modern social atmospheres, etc. (just as we usually see in relation to the so-called developed countries) of many sub-Sahara African countries was shown around the world, it would trigger a more positive and receptive global attitude, which could in turn elevate the perception of Africa to a higher level.

Disheartening enough, it is a fact that many communities in sub-Saharan Africa do indeed have such positive developments but for obvious deliberate reasons, the international media would rather avoid presenting this, opting for the usual negative pictures and images.

'Why do the international media focus on the negatives in relating to news and information about sub-Saharan Africa and its people?'

This is an issue that has puzzled many of us for a long time. To those of us from countries in sub-Saharan Africa, we are witnesses, as well as integral part of modern communities, completely alien to the majority of people looking in through the lenses of the international media.

Why is it important to the international media to repeatedly present communities they refer to in generalizing terms as "Africa" and "Africans" under primitive conditions; dirt, clay and straw-roof housing, no electricity and running water and bloated-belly tattered kids? What is the 'payoff' for them?

Pictures and images of Nairobi – the capital of Kenya, Accra – the capital of Ghana, the commercial section of Abidjan – the capital of Cote d'Ivoire, Harare – the capital of Zimbabwe, Luanda – the capital of Angola, Dakar – the capital of Senegal and many more can in no doubt be comparable to big internationally known cities in the world like New York, London, Madrid, Paris.

Many might argue as to the relevance of this remark I have made above, and I will say it is extremely relevant to the eventual effect it has on the global view of sub-Saharan Africa and their various communities, directly relating to the perception people have of them and thus, the eventual long-lasting damaging consequences.

Of course not, many communities in the sub-Sahara region of the African continent are quite modern and developed, contrary to the image that has been created through both the conscious and the subconscious efforts of the international media.

The very negative and damaging perception of the various communities in sub-Saharan Africa living in the 'dark ages' is far from the truth. Contrary to the common perception, there are many educational institutions of many levels that cater daily for the schooling and education of many kids and the youth, without it ever being known to the international community. To put it simply, I, along with many others, strongly believe that the international media do not care and are not interested in presenting any other image than that already presented.

As cynical as it might appear and pointed out in other places in this book, I believe whole-heartedly that the negative image of sub-Saharan Africa and its people plays a pivotal role in the way people around the world views themselves and live their lives. Unless the international media is confronted with this issue, this very conscious, biased, and unfair treatment that is given to the sub-Saharan Africa and its people will never change. I am rather concerned about the potential for it to get worse with each passing day, week, month, and year, which will have dire consequences for many generations to come.

A very well edited documentary film was shown on TV a couple of evenings ago. The title of this documentary is 'Poverty, Inc.' (Poverty, Incorporated) and it documents an extensive appalling state of events involving the "poor people" of this world and the rest of the world, especially the donor countries and the numerous Aid/Humanitarian organizations.

Though with this documentation of what I refer to as 'crime against humanity', I would respectfully excuse myself from taking up the burden of all the poor people of this world, and concentrate on that of those from sub-Sahara region of the African continent.

It is no puzzle for some of us to come to the understanding of the role played by poor and deprived people from sub-Saharan Africa and especially that by the aid and humanitarian organizations. It is a thriving profitable business kept in motion by the exceptional roles consciously played by the international media, and I often wonder as to why no one from some of the powerful media networks and organizations has made a remark about it. Is it because it has been accepted as a norm, or it is because there are some hidden agendas involved?

With every passing minute, the multi-billion industry of holding the poor very poor, undermines the true essence of life itself for many and how the international community does nothing to combat it is beyond my basic understanding.

My observation is that the aid organizations have serious personal interests in maintaining the presentation of the people from the various communities in sub-Saharan Africa as poor as possible. Aid and humanitarian organizations, with the direct assistance from the international media, indulge in what I refer to as the 'poverty exhibitionism' in order to raise money to finance their agendas. In their aggressive efforts to access monetary donations for their diverse operations, humiliating, degrading, demeaning, and abominable images of sub-Saharan Africa and its people are regularly depicted via the international media by the aid and humanitarian organizations.

It is common knowledge to the world that these aid and humanitarian organizations offer the assistance they do because they care about "Africa and Africans," and I am sure this intent is definitely genuine but their actions say otherwise, and I do not waiver in my strong belief of this being far from the truth. The actions, some of which are mentioned above, by the aid and humanitarian organizations aided by the international media, clearly disregards the essence of human dignity for the dark-skin sub-Sahara African. They just do not care about the dignity of the "Africans".

The methods used in portraying the sub-Saharan Africa region and its communities are to some of us very unfair, but to the many in the international community, it is a good gesture. This is, of course, notwithstanding the negative consequences it has had and still has. The only exposure of sub-Saharan Africa and its people to the international community is that of the images that are presented daily via the media, thus, denying them the opportunities accessible to them, just as it is for many others around the world.

There are very clear discriminatory practices on the part of the international media which I am sure is no big news to those of us who know but not to the great majority around the world; the image of degradation, desperation, helplessness, and all the rest that follows are too deeply imprinted in their minds, making it easy for the international media not to change their ways, and conveniently capitalized on by the aid and humanitarian organizations.

There are countless positive developments in the various communities in sub-Saharan Africa, individually and collectively but this is not in the interest of those who benefit from the status quo of Africa as presented for decades.

The international media has the means and resources to embark on a more positive contribution to the image and pictures they have helped present over many years. They could start by de-mystifying the continent of Africa and the communities in the sub-Saharan region by investing in efforts to do away with their egos and educating themselves about the dark-skin citizens and cease their all-too-familiar generalization, which in turn gives credence to the negative image. With the means and resources available to the various media networks and the ever-growing Information Technology, it should be no problem.

'What should it take,' I have often wondered, for the powerful and influential international media to tell the world about the diversities in cultures, characters, traditions, religions, and languages between Gambia in West Africa and Kenya in East Africa, between Ghana and Nigeria both in West Africa, between the Republic of South Africa and Namibia, Zimbabwe and Somalia, even neighboring countries like Tanzania and Mozambique, or Angola and Zambia?

Just like it is in Europe and elsewhere other than with the African continent, it would seem out of place for the international media to confuse the identities of various independent countries in relation to either a positive or negative news or information. I cannot imagine the international media focusing or even mentioning any unproductive and negative news originating from one or multiple European countries (no matter their border or close international relationship is), as being a collective European issue. This as we all know, is important to the image presented to the societies outside world, which is essential in the presentation and maintenance of the said country.

It must be important for the American, the English, the German, the French, the Canadian, the Danish, the Swedish, the Dutch, the Belgian, the Brazilian, the Mexican, the Japanese, the Chinese, the Saudi Arabian, the Kuwaiti, the Egyptian, the light-skin South African, and many more, to have and feel a strong sense of pride for being who they are, in all that is positive and dignifying as a human being.

In my often wild escapism into the world of wishful thinking, I have experienced the sudden attraction and interest from the international community for the various communities and countries in sub-Saharan Africa and the positive outcome it has had for the entire people in the region with, of course, the massive efforts by the international media.

In thinking of tourism and the huge foreign currency profits it generates for many countries and societies around the world and as expected, with the conscious assistance of the international media by their gracious ability to promote the said countries through presenting the positive sides, there are so many interesting, beautiful and captivating things to see and experience in sub-Saharan Africa for people who visit many of the communities.

Without having anything against animal lovers and animal activists, animals have for many years been the attraction for many visiting the continent of Africa, without any positive regards for the humans. Through my lenses, I have for a long time come to terms with the cynical idea that the welfare of animals supersedes that of humans.

I take my hat off for all the efforts put in by animal activists and animal lovers and not forgetting the immense role played, as usual, by the international media, without whom such efforts would be fruitless. In another twist of cynicism, I can shamelessly say that from the look of things over a very long time, the existence of the animals in many parts of sub-Saharan Africa has been a very big integral part of their economies. In other words, the source of revenue supporting the human existence of many of the communities down in sub-Saharan Africa has been based on the existence of the animals made known to the communities outside of the African continent by the international media. In trying to sum up all of the above and from the human point of view, animals are apparently the clear benefits of the image that has been un-voluntarily planted in peoples' minds with the help of the international media.

Some historical facts could be established which could positively affect the worldwide perception of sub-

Saharan Africa and with it, a portion of the deserved respect.

Between the 5th and 15th centuries, the economies of Europe needed serious boost and communities in Africa were instrumental in establishing trade routes across the Mediterranean to the Italian city of Venice. The main product which was traded in, that acted as an injection to the then depleted European economy, was gold from the West African Kingdoms like the old Ghana, Mali, Senegal, and Niger to the north through the Sahara, establishing the famous caravan routes. This trade route, which functioned for 1,000 years, was essential in the rise of the economy of Europe, and it could be news that the international media could choose to present now and then, to positively affect the image of especially the sub-Saharan Africa, the same way they have contributed negatively.

The BBC's (British Broadcasting Corporation) contribution to the ignorance and the negative perception of the dark-skin people from the various societies in sub-Saharan Africa is so widely exhibited even in these modern times through their natural programs, in which no matter their fascinating presentation of these their popular programs, there is always an element or more of their negative and demeaning connotations regarding the inhabitants of the said country and countries.

I recently saw a BBC TV documentary on a 'Wildlife and Nature' program hosted by the famous Sir David Attenborough, superbly displaying his usual flair and elaborated work dedicated to unraveling the myths surrounding two of the animals in the wild from the African and South American continents. It was rather fascinating and I, for one, could not help myself wonder over why the same could not have been done for the dark-skin population from sub-Saharan Africa, who for centuries have had their existence surrounded by myths and misunderstandings, contributing immensely to the current negative state in which they find themselves in and perceived by the world at large.

Chapter 5
The African

Who is an African? What do we understand by the
reference of the person African? Do we really know who
an African really is? How many of us have given this
subject any thought? As mentioned in the early chapter, it
looks to me that the expressions – 'African and Africa'
comes so easy to each one of us, so easy that we have
never bothered to make any effort to know. Why should
we? Or should we?

All who originate from countries that make up the
African continent have a legitimate reason to identify
themselves as an African, or be referred to as such but in
what way can they lay credence to this?

Being an African is more of a definition imposed on
the dark-skin population of the independent nations on
the continent and by far, it is an acceptable position taken
by the entire world, including, unfortunately, some
citizens from countries in sub-Saharan Africa. I have
often heard the police put out an alert on a wanted person
whose description is none other than the wanted, to be
'an African'. This, I must say, has always prompted me
into calling the TV stations, radio stations, and some of
the traditional print news media, presenting my query as
to the meaning of their broadcast which they claim is on

behalf of the police. Is the wanted person 'an African' because he or she is of a dark-skin complexion, or of a specific build, look, attitude? What really defines "an African"?

As elaborated in subsequent sections of this book, being 'an African' has long been an identity for people for whom no specific bearing is given.

Interestingly, in consulting with the dictionary for the meaning of "an African", the following are given as by the British as an adjective – '*denoting or relating to Africa or any of its peoples, languages, nations, etc.*'

The same source has as nouns – 1) '*a native inhabitant, or citizen of any of the countries of Africa,*' and 2) '*a member or descendant of any of the peoples of Africa, especially a black person.*'

Another given meaning from the same dictionary is an adjective – '*Also Africa; of or from Africa, belonging to the black peoples of Africa,*' and as nouns – '*a native or inhabitant of Africa/ (loosely) a black or another person of African ancestry.*' The origin of the name, reference, identity, word, or whatever one chooses to call this, is Latin and Greek!

Long before the white men set foot on the continent of Africa, there were kingdoms, empires, tribal denominations, religions, histories that clearly defined the individual and people collectively. The people identified themselves to the exclusivity of the others, either through their social and community set-ups. Just as it is elsewhere in the world, the differences between the various communities were established and respected.

So, where and when did the name, word or expression "African" come from?

I know from written historical information that an African is an inhabitant and descendant of people who originate from the African continent and it goes further to clearly state a distinctive difference in the reference to this name, word, expression, or whatever it intended to be, which is: the color of the skin – being dark, or black in complexion.

So, therefore, to be an African, you must have a dark or a black skin complexion. Or is it so? Is the name, term or reference "African" founded to fit particular people and not necessarily the geographic orientation? If not so, I do not understand why, for as long as I can remember, some other people who also originate from societies on the African continent are not referred to as Africans.

Images and pictures of an African, from as far back as when I was a preteen was and still looks a certain way. Judging from the attitudes of a majority (including surprisingly, many from communities on the African continent) whose perception I believe has been influenced by the same images and pictures.

Looking back in history, images, pictures, illustrations, and the definition of who an African is, has been and still is, is that of a person of dark-skin complexion, 'uncivilized', 'primitive', and 'uncultivated'. I have, as an interesting personal experiment, asked some people randomly about their definition of an African, and though the responses and reactions differed in a wide spectrum, there was not a single one I would otherwise consider positive. In some instances, there was a clear conflict of the perception of the continent Africa and the person African. It was obvious that the definition of an African was either overshadowed by the perception of the continent or the reverse. It is so clear and rightly so in my opinion, that people's perception and conclusion is based on a serious lack of knowledge and information. This conclusion of mine might in some way come out as being unfair to the majority who are simply concluding based on the only information they know or have known which is usually through the media.

We all know from our school days that learning about other people, other cultures, other societies, and other places than our own is mostly through academic learning, therefore, my conclusion is that the perception most people have is what has been taught to them by their tutors or teachers, who have in turn been taught by tutors and teachers before them.

The puzzle is in trying to find out the real reason behind the name African, who introduced that word or name, and the meaning of the name. This, of course, has been triggered by the constant negativity connected with the name "African" for so many years.

My early recollection of the broader understanding of who an African is, was my introduction to the 'literature of slavery' that I read in a school class. The main interest of the white man was to capture Africans and take them away from their homes into slave castles and then transport them by sea to the Americas. The slave was a possession of the slave master, who had the power and freedom to do whatever he or she wanted to do with the slave.

The sketchy illustrations of black boys, men, girls, and women in a line formation, bound together by chains around their necks, ankles, and hands tied behind their backs, and seemingly escorted by a couple of armed white guards of some sort, apparently on their way to the slave castles after being captured.

Chapter 6
Colonization – The Vestiges

The vast continent of Africa – the second biggest, I would say, is most probably the richest of all continents in terms of its rich natural resources and with a population of over 1.2 billion, also in human resources. It has all the riches that a man could wish for; fertile land for agriculture, gold, crude oil, diamonds, manganese, bauxite, copper, and much more. In terms of the diverse vegetation and geographical positions as well as the diverse climates which contribute to the enormous wealth.

Could this be interesting for perhaps some people who have in their nature to explore both their near and far surroundings? History and time has been a teaching tool for us to know that the need and quest for physical wealth in terms of riches can easily be a strong catalyst for humans to migrate from one area to another, not forgetting the need for a better life.

The timeline of historical events involving the continent of Africa and Africans in general clearly shows the beginning and events of the European imperialist's aggressive surge onto the continent of Africa. In referring to the historical timeline, this new aggressive migration onto the African continent was from 1870, shortly after the official abolition of the slave trade which, as indicated, was in 1860. It is important to mention that the official records for the period of the slave trade show that for well over 350 years (1500 – 1860), the capture and sale of Africans with dark-skin complexion formed the foundation of many economies in Europe and elsewhere. The mention of this historical fact is to underline the importance of the role the "African" played as a commodity for the establishments of economies in Europe, and the Americas, and therefore, might have been worrying for the Europeans who then had to find ways of sustaining their economies.

From the 1870s – 1900s, it is obvious in realizing that a very significant and important part of the foundation, which supported the feeding of their economies, was derailed. The Europeans, in what must have been an act of desperation, had to find a way to substitute this seemingly lucrative venture that the now abolished slave trade must have provided them and therefore, another chapter of human cruelty in history on the continent of Africa transpired for decades. The vestige of colonization has, without a doubt, had a deeply rooted negative influence in the thinking, culture, traditions, and way of lives of especially citizens of countries in sub-Saharan Africa, even to this present day.

In my search to find and understand the reasons for the continuous apparent perception of special rights by Europeans, especially, that the African continent and its inhabitants are subject to the European domain and influence, plus, the absurd conclusion of ownership to execute those rights lead me to some rather interesting revelations so visible and influential in various communities across sub-Sahara African countries.

Among the motivating factors that initiated the aggressive march by the Europeans into Africa are economic, social and political, the ones I consider most strong. To uphold such agenda as a means to their final goal, the Europeans resorted to pressures in different tactical forms, including diplomacy, military, even religious, and others reflective of imperialist campaigns to achieve their goal; colonization, which they eventually did. Despite the various small and large pockets of resistance put up in different African countries, the imperial dominant power succeeded in establishing their bases across a very big percent of the African continent, and thereby colonies belonging to various European countries had been soundly established by the time the 1900s started.

With all the reasons and excuses, characteristic of Capitalist exploiters, the European colonial Imperialist, in every effort to fill in the massive hole left by the missing revenues from the abolished slave trade and in pretending to care, presented other possibilities to their subjects, amongst which were the availabilities of schooling, training, jobs, as well as other seemingly attractive possibilities to better their lives.

The continent of Africa being rich in natural resources, including a vast variety of raw materials needed by the Europeans to support their ambitious plans of expanding their industrial revolution, which as mentioned earlier, is one of the real reasons for the European colonial Imperialist expansion. The strong need to secure and guarantee constant access to the valuable raw materials in Africa which supports the ambitious Capitalist Industrial Revolution and plus, the important securing and protection of their markets and investments, clearly makes their economic interest the leading motivating factor.

It is paramount to note that the struggle for dominance in Africa by the European colonial Imperialists was fueled apparently by the competitive race among themselves for power and the establishment of superior stature in Europe. The race to acquire new territories was a form of expanding their domains as well as having the edge over each other within the competing powers in Europe, and the possibility of dividing the various African countries in a calculative manner became a goal. The English, the French, the Swedes, the Danes, the Portuguese, the Spanish, the Italians, the Belgians and the Germans, all played significant roles in colonizing the continent of Africa and its people, some more than others. It is evident that the European Imperialists had no intention of loosening their grip on Africa and the African societies, not only to manifest their perception of superiority over their subjects on the African continent even after the abolition of the slave trade, colonization had to quickly be set in motion.

The arrival of the European Imperialist into Africa and the establishment of their colonial rules and governments gave birth to the demise of most of the self-governing Kingdoms that served the various communities across the continent, uprooting and destroying the foundations; some very ancient, on which many of the communities were built and replacing them with their own, which they forced onto the Africans and into the

African societies without regard for the impending short and long-term effects it would have on the entire continent. The sometimes fierce resistance put up against the introduced European Imperialist systems by the Africans, though often discarded in biased historical documentation, did very little to prevent what I personally consider the most abominable act in all of the colonial periods to date, and the atrocious manners they introduced, which has had a severe lasting effect on the African continent, especially in the sub-Saharan region, and can both easily be seen and strongly felt in the various communities.

The birth of the industrial revolution which had started in Britain had gained momentum and spread to other parts of Europe; France, Belgium, Germany, and to the United States of America, which also brought with it massive social challenges. Life for the poor and working classes continued to be filled with challenges. In the early 1860s, industrialization had meant that lots of craftsmen and craftswomen were replaced by machines, resulting in the urban and industrial areas attracting many workers from the countryside. The results were that of living conditions that were unsanitary, inadequate, overcrowded and polluted housing facilities which bred rampant diseases. The transition from pre-industrialized to industrialized Britain, especially, creating social inequalities and comprising more of farming communities with very meager income, brought with it massive social problems unparalleled to any before. Unemployment grew at a fast rate and people became poor and homeless. The reputation of Britain being the birthplace of the industrial revolution in maintaining as well as sustaining the status of a stable society is closely tied to its ambitions, which was to keep and uphold this position among other imperialist invaders on the African continent. Before long, Britain will execute its ambitious plan to attain the position as the leading colonial power by way of the vicious campaign in its established colonies on the African continent from where it had secured the source for the vital raw materials, as well as a marketplace for the goods they eventually manufactured.

In their relentless quest for power and dominance, the European Imperialists, who were themselves dealing with inter-nation supremacy and competition for political power, ceased the opportunity of free access made available through the 'buffet' status, at the time presented by the crushing of the African resistance, gathered to convene a historic meeting with a goal in mind; possibly, their efforts to ward off fears of conflicts and even wars between the imperialists looming over them; the concern for the fierce competition to win as many territories as possible. In the latter parts of 1884 and about 3 months on, the then German Chancellor – Otto von Bismarck organized and called for a high-level meeting amongst the diplomats of the European imperial powers, which came to be known generally as the 'Berlin Conference'. The apparent purpose of this meeting was to address the concerns, some which are mentioned immediately above, and come to an understanding, leading to the formation of the treaty known as the 'Berlin Act.'

Under this treaty, understandings and agreements were made on the code of conducts and guidelines for the European imperialist invaders, not so much on how to govern their subjects on the African continent but rather, the provisions made available on how to conduct and control themselves in light of the competition they faced collectively between themselves.

It is important to note, the formation of this treaty has no involvement or inclusion of anyone from the African continent and neither has the place of the treaty agreement any relation to the African continent! It is also worth mentioning that this treaty made available the later occurrence of invasion, separation of communities and the eventual colonization of the African continent by the European imperialists.

The essence of this treaty comprised of a number of significant articles defining certain principles such as a) making each other/others aware of their annexing the various territories and validating these annexations through occupation. b) Unchallenged liberty to do trading in certain geographical areas on the African continent and the same liberty to trade with other nations and c) putting an end to the slave trade commerce, both by land and sea, are some worth mentioning.

In my cautious understanding of such developments and my interpretation of the variety of documented historical literature and as expected, a degree of resistance was fiercely consequently displayed by the various African kingdoms and sub-states towards the European intended take-over of their lands and imposing colonial rule on them. This is manifested in the aftermath of this infamous (for Africans) treaty in Berlin – 'Berlin Act', – when conflicts arose due to the different understandings from the interpretations on both sides when representatives of the European imperialist invaders followed up on the treaty and traveled to meet up with the Africans to consummate it.

The gap between the Europeans and Africans in relation to how this treaty was interpreted and understood was so wide that serious conflicts were inevitable. It also demonstrated the characters of these two peoples, which in more ways than one, is so evident even to this present day. The European imperialist invaders had concluded that these treaties signed between themselves and the Africans meant that full sovereign rights had been relinquished to them and had every intention to execute their plans of annexation of territories, domination and colonizing, while the Africans had concluded the treaties to be more of a friendship and diplomatic relationships for commercial purposes. The revelation of the real intent of the Europeans became self-evident to the Africans soon after, who then developed mistrust towards the Europeans. Tensions built up, leading to a militarily organized African resistance.

The African resistance, which was in the form of kingdoms, empires, and other small-scale local based powers from within the centralized state systems, had armies capable of engaging the Europeans troops with masses of their own.

Some of such African military resistance put up worth a mention was those by the Zulu kingdom of Southern Africa, the Mandinka of West Africa, The Ashanti kingdom of modern day Ghana, the Igbos of Nigeria, and the Ethiopians. The Ethiopians, however, led by a very strong and determined military leader in the person of Menelik II, succeeded in their fierce resistance against the imperial invader – Italy. From the 1890s,

Ethiopia succeeded in resisting the massive pressure to impose colonial rule on them mounted by Italy. It is recorded that in the famous battle of 1896, Ethiopian troops of a 100,000 inflicted a significant defeat on the Italians and maintained thereon, its independence for much of the colonial rule period, except during the pause from between 1936 and 1941 due to the Italian supervision.

The military forces organized by various African societies against the invading European imperialist forces put up very stiff resistance in diverse ways but had to capitulate in the end. Many reasons have been given through time but the most credible, in my opinion, is that of the huge difference in the technology of warfare which was available at that time.

Whereas the Africans resorted to the weapons they knew well (which would be considered primitive); bows and arrows, spears, swords, and other locally made items of diverse forms used during their own inter-kingdom, inter-tribal and interstate wars of the past, the Europeans utilized the fruits of the labor put in their Industrial Revolution, allowing them access to more superior weapons and more-than-enough firepower to crush the African resistance, whose frantic efforts were to stop their societies from being colonized. Ultimately, the Africans succumbed to the European imperialist invasion, due not only to their inferior warring conditions compared to that of the opposition but due also in part to the disorganization and internal rifts within the various communities in diverse dimensions and in spite of their heroic efforts, the African communities were "devoured by the colonial powers".

By 1900, the colonial powers had cemented their holds on their new territories and domains in Africa. The dim historical foundations and time for total exploitation of natural and human resources of people had been laid out, with the main architects being the British, the French, the Belgians, the Spanish, the Portuguese, the Germans, and the Italians. It is well noting that the Danes, Swedes, and the Dutch had as well played significant roles in their historically atrocious acts which seems irrelevant in these times in terms of the effects it has on humanity.

The immediate realism of postcolonial Africa after their defeat to the European imperialist was to witness the complete dismantle of their ways of governance in diverse forms by the various communities and replaced by that which gave full and outright power to the European imperial invaders.

In as much as efforts are being made to either avoid or minimize 'racism' relating to this subject as well as others in this book being a significant theme, it is inevitable to separate the obvious underlining ideology motivating the European imperialist invaders, which is racism. The colonial powers inevitably setup their systems comprising primarily of Administrative organs which should help assist the progress of the control and the effective exploitation of their colonized societies.

As expected, the colonial powers did not have the full support of their subjects in the established colonial states in which governance was bureaucratic and authoritarian. This was because the African subjects of these colonial governments were not made part of the decision-making apparatus they were governed under and therefore, never consented to the legitimacy of these colonial governments. Duties and various tasks got accomplished through bureaucratic and authoritarian processes due to the direct involvement of the military and locals appointed by the colonial governments.

Fierce resistance to the setups of these colonial rules in the new territories and colonial states was put up by the subjects of these European imperial invaders. These resistances came in different forms and by different states. There were political resistance and other forms of military resistances put up from different parts of the continent. Some of the resistances against the colonial rule that standout are those that took place in three states from the West African region. Against the British Imperialist invaders, the Igbos of Southeastern Nigeria utilized their knowledge of the terrain and using the guerrilla tactic, made it difficult for the British. Though the British officially colonized the Igbos after 1902, events proved that it was more of a partial victory as the Igbos continued their sporadic resistant actions in the territory long after.

The story of the female leader of the Ashanti Empire of present-day Ghana is another. Yaa Asantewaa led a mobilized resistance against British colonialism in what is known in history as 'the Yaa Asantewaa War', also as 'the Ashanti Uprising', 'the Third Ashanti Expedition', and 'the War of the Golden Stool'. They put up a resistance against the Ashanti Empire being colonized and the surrender of the 'Golden Stool' (which was the throne and a symbol of Ashanti sovereignty). This was one war among many conflicts that they had against the British Imperial Government of the then Gold Coast.

A third known resistance which was against the French imperialists was by the Mandinka Empire in West Africa, organized and led by Samory Toure. In a period of 16 years (between 1882 and 1898), Samory Toure and his people put up perhaps, the strongest of all the resistant movements against colonial rule, using many tactics which the French imperialists found difficult to break. The Mandinka Empire resistance included an intelligent means of acquiring firearms (from European Traders in other West African states), as well as places where firearms were repaired and manufactured in small scale. Samory Toure's relentless resistance against the French imperialists embodied well-trained forces whose motivation was strengthened by the sheer determination to defend their nation to fullest against being colonized.

A very important observation I have made in most of the sub-Saharan African countries is the clarity of the effect the colonial period has had on the various communities in these countries, which are without doubt closely connected to a significant legacy of colonial rule.

Though the pattern and forms of administrative systems in the various colonial states were more or less uniform; authoritarian, bureaucratic and often inhumane, it was visible to see the differences amongst them, due interestingly to the political orientation of the different European colonial national administrative traditions and the conditions politically of the territories under their domains. In other words, the administration by the colonized states differed based on the political traditions of the different European colonial rulers and reflecting their specific imperial ideologies and due to the political conditions in the colonized states.

The legacies of Colonial rule can be seen and felt all across the African continent but in some more than others. The French influence in their territories on the African continent is an example so clear even to this day and in no way comparable to the others. They set up a strong administrative system which was centralized and strongly influenced by their ideology of colonialism and fully stated claims of being on a mission to civilize the natives and lift them out of their 'intellectual retard' status and making them into civilized Africans; Africans of French orientation, or French Africans.

The mechanism put in place for executing the governance of their colonies in Africa was somehow intricate, despite the original intent of the European imperialist invaders of exporting their democracy to their newly acquired colonies. Democracies, based on the consent of the governed, would not have created the problems and opposition the European Colonialists eventually faced.

The modus operandi of the colonial rules for governing in their colonies differed in some ways. The majority of the new colonies were of either British or the French influence, with a few being that of the others. The British system of government was by a centralized power-based model, ruling by the division of administrative duties from the top down. This system of government was established in their colonies from the West; the Gold Coast (modern-day Ghana), Nigeria, Kenya, Uganda, Tanganyika (modern-day Tanzania) to the east. An appointed Governor and executive council governed together and plus, a council of lawmakers made up of both local and foreign members, usually from the colonial capitals. Political programs, policies and laws were sent from the colonial secretariat with offices located in London down to the Governor who had the overall responsibilities and authority to make and influence the local laws and policies, apart from the colonial directives and policies whose implementations were via a centralized administrative organ within the colonial secretariat who then delegates the various functions to the appropriate departments like Education, Health, Transport, Tax, Mining, Agriculture, etc.

In order for the European imperialist invaders to fortify their status and secure the guarantee for the continuous benefits from their established territories on the continent of Africa, they needed the complete loyalty of their subjects, so they embarked on transforming them, one way or the other.

This was notable more especially with the French, who unlike the British as mentioned above, had a different approach worth pointing out.

As briefly mentioned above, the French took an approach of assimilation of its colonial subjects from Tunisia, Algeria in the northern part, to Senegal, Cote d'Ivoire, Cameroon in the west, to mention a few. The French saw the natives as primitive, uncultured and uncivilized, and therefore, made it their mission to turn the natives into a more acceptable French way of thinking and living. This, in the eyes of the French, was more of a civilized way unlike the 'intellectually retarded' way of life lead by their subjects in the colonies. The assimilation policy embarked upon by the French was executed through education, culturalization, and hoping that the natives would undergo some sort of metamorphosis to become cultured and civilized 'French-Africans'. Though history tells us of the plans of the French colonial invaders had for their colonies and subjects on the African continent, it is obvious they had little or no intention of really making their subjects, the French citizens, as themselves. They went on and implemented some plans and conditions to thwart all attempts by their subjects to become full French citizens, like a requirement to speak the French language fluently, services rendered to the French colonial government deserving praise, and other strange conditions.

Among some of the reasons why the natives aimed at acquiring full French citizenship was this very absurd rule; the rights accompanying French citizenship, of being covered and tried applying the French judicial process within the French Courts of law instead of the native's, which is otherwise based on the indoctrination and legal practices of the French colonial rulers. A subject of the French colonies was denied the rights to the official French legal due-process, and instead, could be tried by the local colonial representatives or their military and subjected to a period of forced labor.

In the era of their colonial rule, the French applied direct rule, which was built on administrative directives, policies, and laws being given directly from Paris to their appointed governors in the capitals of their colonies in the north, west and in central Africa, to be enforced locally in accordance with those applied in France.

In reflecting on the colonial period on the African continent, it is not complicated to see traces of the various colonial practices and methods, as well as legacies deeply planted in the various communities. The two dominating and major powers; the French with their direct rule whose effects are ever so present even to this day and the official national language which is, of course, French, strongly downplaying the role played by the various tribal languages and maintaining the primal influence from Paris, often overriding local thinking, even politically, despite them having secured their independence from France many years back.

The influence of the British colonial period with their indirect rule has not been deeply rooted in their colonies as much as it has with especially the French, however, the bureaucratic administrative system still casts its shadows in the modern time independent former subjects. The language, judicial, educational and political administrations are manifested in the daily operations at both local and national levels of societies.

The influences of the other European colonial powers; Portugal, Belgium, Germany, Italy, and Spain, have different impacts on the colonies today, even after many years of gaining independence. The languages, administration in different sectors of government and cultures are all signs of the magnitude mental adaptation of the colonial rule have on the African continent. Though different in their approach, their goals were the same; take over a people by force for exploitation at all levels and by all means necessary, to serve a selfish imperialistic purpose without regard for the effect on humanity.

Chapter 7
The Myths

I am from a tribe in Ghana called 'Ashanti', which is definitely a significant and dominating tribe with a very rich culture and history dating many centuries back. The Ashanti tribe is very significant in the shaping of the modern day Ghana, due also to the crucial roles it played during and after the colonial era. The Ashanti people are a proud people, fearless by birth, rich in natural resources, with the particular mention of gold, and above all, very proud of their culture.

History has recorded the fierce resistance and revolt by the Ashanti people against the various colonial powers in protecting their cultural heritage. The same history tells of the heroic manifestations of different kinds of the Ashanti people in fiercely defending their territories against the colonial powers and one of these stories make mention of a woman by the name of Yaa Asantewaa, who led the Ashanti forces against a British force in one of the wars that took place during the colonial era.

The need for my mentioning of this story is to try to relate to readers the sense of independence, self-reliance and huge pride of a people independent of any outside influence and yet, there is a very significant reference made about a song which used to be sung by the older generation of Ashanti women in some form of a ritual ceremony of happiness.

'If you are looking for God and you cannot find him, turn to the White Man' is the song of praises sung during these ritual ceremonies. Be it true or false, it is by no means a clear depiction of the state of mind of the majority of our locals who are considered illiterates and sadly, I must add, some literates as well.

It should be some sort of a wonder but seriously, I do not think it is the case either for the "White Man", or for the majority of the local "African" people.

'Why should it be?' I ask.

Many years ago, I invited my then girlfriend of mixed race (having parents being black and white) on a visit to Ghana, and she was elated by such an invitation. I will never forget when she told me of the reaction of her colleagues at work who were predominantly Whites. Her reception of their reactions and comments were that of mixed feelings. On one part they were happy for her pending trip to Africa, and on the other hand, they were concerned about her 'survival' and eventual return to Denmark. A particular concern of her colleagues, which was made known on repetitive occasions at her workplace, was that of her sleeping arrangements upon arrival in Ghana. Though many years have passed by since this episode and we are in the year 2012, I must shamefully admit on behalf of my fellow human beings outside of the African continent, that this myth of Africans sleeping up in trees is only strengthened by the continuous portrayal of the "African" and the African continent. Her colleagues were seriously demanding to know whether she was going to spend some sleeping hours, whiles in Ghana, in the bushes, up in trees or in smoke-filled-run-down mud huts. There are still some who sincerely believe that "Africans" are monkeys, and or directly related to monkeys, therefore, it was no surprise for her colleagues to think that way. I would bet that even my girlfriend, without displaying her reactions to the concerns of her colleagues, most probably had wondered likewise.

I remember laughingly suggesting to my girlfriend some days after our arrival in Ghana, to climb up into a tree which was decoratively planted in front of our 4-star international hotel, permitting me to take picture of her with the sarcastic intent to show her colleagues back in Denmark when she arrived back home. I must admit, the interest I had in knowing the reactions of her colleagues was overshadowed by the concerns of the effects of such beliefs the 'outside world' has of "Africans".

Being a sports enthusiast, a great deal of my spare time is spent at various sporting events around the world. This can be attributed primarily to my background, from my youth as an active sportsman, even to this day. All sporting events usually catch my attention; watching live, via television, different internet media, and of course, via the various news networks.

As exhibited in nature, I believe in the division of abilities of all creations, be it individually or collectively, to engage and in some instances, strive for excellence and success. One area where the efforts and positive results of Africans are documented is in the field of sports. Participating and competing amongst others is a catalyst by which every human being has the opportunity to demonstrate his or her abilities.

In track and field, football/soccer, to mention a few, Africans have been engaging and excelling in some instances. The need to compete and win is an ambition that has been demonstrated amongst humans of all origins and backgrounds for generations of the past as well as those of the present, and people from the sub-Saharan region of the African continent are no different. I have often heard from the experts, commentators, and enthusiasts on diverse sporting events which have had Africans excelling, comments indicating that certain attributes have definitely been the motivating factor for those particular successes; a significant one being poverty. Because the kids from Africa are poor and need to excel in order to earn recognition and the benefits thereafter so as to provide for the families who depend on them, thus, they tend to do better than the kids who are well off. In agreeing partially to a good economic and financial base being a possible factor to succeed at whatever 'the African' is engaged in, it is a deliberate misconception that this factor is exclusive to African sports participants alone. The British, the German, the American, Russian, Chinese, etc. would want to succeed and excel where necessary, just as much as

'the African'. Paradoxically, the rise to prominence, economic and financial gain is, without a doubt, the motivating factor for the 'non-African' to compete and excel as well, just as it is for the rest of the world. I would further state, though, that the world's conception of Africa and Africans, and including the dehumanization thereof, is definitely a major contributing factor for par excellence in their endeavors.

Still, in the sports genre, I find it grotesque, tasteless and mean when the so-called experts conclude that the ultimate dream and goal for the African football/soccer players is to gain access via professional contracts to ply their trades in the lucrative clubs abroad, especially in Europe.

'Is it not the dream, aspiration and goal of all other players to gain access to lucrative clubs in Europe as well?' I ask myself whenever I come across such statements. Though European players ply their trades in possibly their home countries, their federation might not be that lucrative and therefore it is a very normal practice for players to seek engagements with other more ambitious and economically sound European clubs. Seeking a better economically financially sound European club, to gain and improve economically and financially, is not an aspiration reserved for Africans alone as it's been presented, but for all around the world, irrespective of their geographic and demographic backgrounds.

Completely disregarding an important known factor being a strong catalyst among many human beings in their endeavors to achieve success and reach their goals, I have often heard the 'experts' (in what I refer to as gross disrespect for hard work) conclude in ways that can only be that based on guesswork, as it usually is, in dealings with Africa. As far as I can remember, athletes from the eastern part of the African continent have had a unique ability paralleled to none in the competitive middle to long distance running events. To name some, Kenyans and Ethiopians are known to excel in big international athletic competitions like the Olympic Games, World

Championships, and other less known competitions. Having my roots in an African country, it is a known fact to me and I am sure to many as well, of the diverse human capabilities we all possess, mainly, but not necessarily exclusive to the geographic dispositions on the continent.

One of the reasons given by those who claim to know the reasons for such dominant successful feat by athletes from eastern part of Africa in middle and long distance athletic competitions, is the natural challenge posed to them from infancy regarding their needs to commute daily between home and school, which should automatically be over very long distances. Such conclusions, I guess, is based on the automatic notion that coming from Africa, there will, of course, be no form of automated transportation like cars, buses, trains, etc. (as known apparently in non-African countries) which could be utilized by these athletes and therefore, the conclusion as given immediately above. This is, as usual, a total disregard for the individual talent, ability, hard work, and dedication (which is considered the cornerstone for sporting success in non-African countries) these athletes exhibit. I once heard an American man proudly telling a group of people of the apparent reason he believed to be the underlining factor for the success in middle and long distance running by 'the African' runners; 'the daily challenge of hunting and chasing down antelopes on the plains of Africa for their much-needed food for survival being the undisputed factor for their dominance in international athletic competitions.'

I do not know whether the perception amongst people outside sub-Saharan Africa is still that "Africans" in

Africa live in trees. It is not that long ago when I encountered people in some European countries as well as in the United States, making comments of how Africans lived in trees just like monkeys do. As much as I disregard such comments to be that of complete ignorance and foolishness, it quickly dawned on me that such comments were not made simply as a form of provocation but that those people who made such comments did actually believe them to be true. I am inclined to conclude that based on my experience, the greater percentage of beliefs and perceptions based on complete ignorance is still more predominant in the societies traditionally with less contact to sub-Saharan Africa. My observation of this deeply grounded perception by many, of "Africans" living in trees, is without doubt the leading factor for the disrespect and lack of human recognition for Africans and unfortunately, black people in general, bearing in mind that every black is an African in the ignorant minds of those who think as such. It is no coincidence that black football/soccer players are still to this present day, subjected to what has come to be known as "monkey sounds", and the throwing of banana peels onto the pitches from spectators in certain places where they ply their trades. I would confidently claim such attitudes being more a cliché than anything else.

An analogy directly relating to the immediate subject above that has me as opinionated as never before is the recent trend we see documented on a television program called 'tree houses'. Apparently, building houses in trees is something that has been around for years but the interest in Europe has escalated of late. Living in tree

95

houses is an old tradition practiced by some societies in the South Pacific region, and I do not recollect this tradition as being looked down on.

The biggest misconception that people have of sub-Sahara Africa and is deeply rooted in the opinions formed is that Africa is poor, making Africans poor by default. This could not be further from the truth. The African continent, which many commonly refer to as "Africa" (most probably due to the little knowledge they have, or lack of it), is very rich. Contrary to popular belief, I dare challenge all who think and make such conclusions in ways detrimental to the respect and growth the continent rightly deserves.

I have often wondered why it is not common knowledge to all of the abundance of wealth available to the inhabitants of the African continent. It is not an exaggeration to conclude that every natural resource that is known to man, and the source of wealth and riches for all communities worldwide, is found on the African continent. The continent of Africa being commonly connected to poverty, degradation, and all the negatives that come with it is not because the continent is poor but rather the mismanagement of the wealth and abundant riches available to them by its inhabitants. The pitiful state in which especially sub-Saharan Africa and its inhabitants finds themselves in is without a doubt, the result of the mismanagement of the wealth and riches by both the inhabitants, as well as foreigners. It is completely wrong to conclude that the state of poverty and all the negatives connected with the image created of Africa is a reflection of the continent being poor.

Reflecting on an important part of my past, I could not forget the very difficult time I had in my relationship with my girlfriend at the time. She was the sweetest I could wish for as a partner; caring, gentle, loving, and full of patience, which is a rare virtue. The relationship between my girlfriend and I was not different than many other romantic relationships between a male and a female, however, I often wondered as to whether my background; being born in Ghana (being African as many would conclude) played a role in the challenges our relationship often faced. I often felt a massive influence in my relationship from her parents and as frustrating as it was, I had no easy way of dealing with it.

My then girlfriend of mixed race and adopted from one European country to another from when she was an infant, though felt very much accepted and welcome by the black community of which I am a part of, automatically had the mentality of 'the white man'. My mention of this is to emphasize the ease with which the influence of the parents on her decision-making concerning our relationship came to bear. It became obvious that whenever she spent time alone with her parents, her attitude towards our relationship was affected in a negative way. I could sense with the passing of time that she doubted the foundation and the future of our relationship. Though I got along well with the parents, I found it odd of her swinging attitude, which included some reckless behaviors unsuitable for a sound romantic relationship. After a lengthy consideration, I gathered the courage to confront her with my concerns, and she then told me about the pressure she had felt from the parents' side that had made her very confused and unsure of our relationship. She told me of the constant message from her parents about how our relationship would not withstand the obvious cultural difference that existed between the two of us. Fortunately and unfortunately, we broke up when she met another man (who happened to be with a white man) introduced to her by her mother.

This experience had a serious effect on my subsequent relationships with other women of the same race and culture as that of the parents of my girlfriend. I had, not before or after, wondered as to the role played by the different cultures in my romantic relationships to the women that had been in my life because though it is a fact of life worth considering, I do not necessarily agree that cultural differences between couples in a romantic relationship are a problem, though it can be. I do not accept, neither do I believe that a romantic relationship of a couple is doomed to fail, especially because one of the partners originates from sub-Sahara Africa. It is short-sightedness to prejudge and conclude that the failure of a relationship between an African and another is due to their cultural orientation, when the failure of other romantic relationships between couples of the same race and culture due exactly to the same cause, is due primarily to inter-human differences.

Has it not been said many times and in many places that schooling of "Africans" will introduce civilization and eliminate poverty in Africa? But it is a known fact, no matter how debatable, that civilization began in Africa, on the African continent, in Egypt? If so, then why should schooling of Africans bring about civilization when it did begin there?

I hear words & sentences like: 'to be cultivated & cultured', 'to be civilized', 'being primitive', how is it like? Is it by doing what is done in Europe, in the US, in South America & elsewhere but in Africa?

'The Dark Continent' is what I remember the continent of Africa being referred to as.

'Why should a continent be called dark?' I have often asked myself.

'Is it a dark continent literarily meant? What are the reasons for such gloomy and depressive labels put on a vast and diverse continent? Has this term been used unfairly for a whole continent of different people, history, religion, beliefs, due to the dark-skin of the inhabitants south of the Sahara?

The continent of Africa is not 'dark' in any form. On the contrary, the various independent countries and communities making up the continent have had, and still have, the brightest opportunities available to all continents on the planet. In terms of natural resources, human resources, development possibilities or educational possibilities, the continent of Africa is very 'bright'.

It is an elusive utopia to conclude that the primary solution for the betterment of the people on the continent of Africa is through academic education. It is no secret that to a large extent, some proposed form of education (referring relatively to the academic form), which I controversially differ in opinion, can and might greatly help. That form of academic education often proposed as a lasting solution for Africa though bears some truth, it's no secret that such act will require so much financing, and where is this type of financing going to come from when citizens of many sub-Sahara African societies have (embarrassingly) no access even to common clean drinking water? It's been said that some wealthy Philanthropists in some parts of the world have thankfully proposed the donation of certain educational tools to help 'the African' kids and students get abreast with the education expected of them. I will respectfully ask how malnourished, hungry, ill-stricken, poor, weak and energy-lacking kids and the youth can be capable of learning anything, no matter the learning tools made available to them.

The so-called 'Experts on Africa' is another serious misunderstanding in my humble opinion.

My understanding of "an expert" on a particular subject is completely different in relation to issues and subjects to do with sub-Saharan Africa and its people. I suppose the criteria used in the determination of the role played by 'an expert' on various issues and subjects differ. My personal opinion on the use of the so-called experts on sub-Saharan Africa issues and subjects is ridiculous. The positions of these so-called experts are usually those other than by the citizens of the said sub-Saharan African country/countries, unlike that, one witnesses in similar situations around the world.

There are those, and many I will believe, who will argue that being an expert on a subject requires an academic knowledge, in other words, reading about the place, people, and things directly relating to the subject and not necessarily physical interaction, which I disagree. In presenting an opinion or making a conclusion on a community in sub-Saharan Africa as it would be for many other communities around the world, I strongly believe that the depth and credibility of the opinions and comments of and from the so-called experts would carry more weight if they had physically been present in the said African community as well as physically interacted with the citizens instead of forming opinions based on reading.

In comparison with a recognized and respected expert's opinion on issues and subjects relating to sub-Saharan Africa, I dare claim that my opinion and comments regarding the Danish society will definitely have with it a great portion of credibility because I have in more ways than one, physically interacted in many ways with the Danes. I have eaten with them, slept with them, played with them, and communicated in different ways with them; I am very much acquainted with the Danish society with such background, than will be had I stayed elsewhere and read about them.

I have never understood why it is acceptable to allow the opinions and comments of the so-called experts on "Africa" (meaning sub-Saharan Africa) and show complete disregard for the people from the sub-Saharan region. It is so apparent that the opinions of the citizens from sub-Sahara African societies have been suppressed and made irrelevant, not by consent but by the obviously acceptable conclusion of being inadequate and incapable of a meaning about their lives, as well as themselves.

The common picture painted out there in the world is that "Africans" do not have the ability, education or intelligence to get themselves out of bad situations, and are always 'bailed out' by everyone else from outside the sub-Sahara region; the Europeans, the North Americans,

South Americans, Australians, Asians, the Japanese, the Chinese, etc.

'The African society is a male-dominated one', many say or perceive. A lot of suggestions have been made over a long period in different forms to assist "Africa" and "Africans" by investing in and empowering the women in the communities. Part of the reason as it is claimed, is that women being the backbone of the growth of societies through their maternal nurturing of children, needs every encouragement and support for a good future of any society; which "Africa", apparently, is certainly not.

Despite the constant bombarding of the immediate above information into our consciousness, I feel a need to make an important remark; a majority of the communities spread across the sub-Saharan Africa region have female or women whose daily functions as matriarchs has steered their communities in the spirit and atmospheres conducive to their environments. Such matriarchal societies in sub-Saharan Africa is an old function of the family life from the village through to the city as well, and it's important to note that this community function is still very much alive even to this day, contrary to the image of the female role being that of a submissive one. Just as I am sure is known through film documentations of different lifestyles of people around the globe, the role of the woman in sub-Saharan Africa can often be that of the bread-winner, heads of the families and in many ways, the ones that undertake many physically-challenging duties otherwise reserved for males.

In this day and age, it might not be relevant to mention this but I want to make it relevant due to its reflection on other aspects of the myth that surrounds the dark-skin people of sub-Saharan Africa. I have often wondered why primates, monkeys and apes are associated with black people from sub-Saharan Africa but quickly came to the realization that these general condescending expressions were not used necessarily in reference to a dark-skin person from a community on the African continent but that it was also used generally by all who felt superior to a black person, irrespective of where they originated from. I dare claim that these rather crude incidents where a dark-skin person from the African continent is referred to as a monkey or an ape, must be due to certainly heated moments where some people of different skin color than black might have used such expression with a retaliatory and vengeful intent, however, there are those who have believed this to be true.

Why the affiliation of apes and monkeys with black people from communities on the African continent? I have for so long wondered as to why. It cannot be for the color because monkeys, apes and primates come in different colors. It cannot be any particular feature on their bodies as the diversity of the apes, monkeys and primates cannot be connected to the features of any black person from communities on the African continent to the exclusivity of any other person anywhere globally.

Therefore, my conclusion is that of creating what is not there and believing in its existence, just like with many other 'make-believe' conclusions relating to sub-Saharan Africa and its communities.

It's no surprise that Africa is synonymous with extreme poverty. This image, as all other images of

Africa, is created by the constant bombardment of degrading and poverty-ridden pictures, especially by the international media to, in my opinion, serve their own selfish purposes. It is necessary for my effort to hopefully start a debate that can shed light as well as provide nuances that can contribute to a fair and rare positive evaluation of the African continent.

I, therefore, ask how Africa must be considered and unfairly judged as being poor when it is a continent blessed with an abundance of riches in forms of natural and human resources. Crude oil, natural gas, gold, diamond, manganese, bauxite, cocoa, coffee, tea, timber, and many more, including some of the newly sought-after natural minerals such as coltan (shortened name for the earthly mineral known as columbite-tantalite), widely used in the manufacture of batteries/electronic products, most notably the modern cell phones and laptops.

The continent of Africa is, without a doubt, the richest continent and the richest landmass which is, unfortunately, mismanaged by the people. The simple conclusion is that Africa is extremely rich, contrary to common perception around the world.

A wide and deep perception by the international community of dark-skin people from sub-Saharan Africa is amongst others, the lack of access to education. It is also part of the deep perception of the outside world that lack of education plays a role in the unfair conclusion of Africa being underdeveloped.

Just as the cradle of civilization is known historically to have been in Egypt and therefore, on the African continent, it is important as well to add that of academic education, contrary to popular perception, has always existed on the African continent and in, indeed, the sub-Saharan Africa.

It is well documented that some of the early institutions of learning were founded on the African continent; in Mali, Morocco, and Egypt. The University of Timbuktu is considered to be one of the early institutions of learning that have existed where many students through time have had their academic tutelage.

Chapter 8
Ignorance

'She should be tied to an aircraft and sent to Africa!!!'
These are the words supposedly uttered by a guy in a
'reality' TV show in an angry reaction to a colleague's
action earlier in the show. Someone called me up on the
phone to tell me about the Danish version of an
international 'Reality' TV shows called 'Paradise Hotel'.
The Danish television channel TV3 seasonally presents
this program whose audience appeal is primarily the
youth between the teen ages up to a maximum of thirty.
Nevertheless, it is known that some adults are wooed into
following this show, often by their daughters. By and
large, I would say that this show appeals more to the
young female audience.

Seriously, how much ignorant can one be, or be given
the benefit of doubt like billions of us on this earth who
know no better?

'I do not believe this,' I said to myself. Is it that bad,
so bad that the name "Africa" is indeed very symbolic
with a place of doom? This is really serious but not
forgetting that this individual, plus a whole lot of others,
need be told that there are millions living on, and, from
the African continent that are better off than he is and
might be having a better life than he cares to know. It (the

African continent south of the Sahara) can indeed be, and is 'paradise' for many.

This TV show whose goal is to entertain, is based on a simple concept of eventual elimination of the participants one after the other until the last person or a couple stands as an eventual winner, which comes with a handsome cash prize.

There are friendly bonds established between participants, back-stabbings, and manipulation of the situations by various participants to their advantage, all with the common goal of becoming eventual winners.

This statement made by this guy in anger as a form of reaction to some act by a fellow participant can only mean one thing to me, and that is that I have wondered many a time when I hear or see any written subject having to do with the continent of Africa – 'Africa must be a place of sufferings, comparable to what we have learnt and been told about hell'.

Why would anybody want another person condemned and sent to Africa as a form of punishment? Why? What could possibly be the reason for this?

The answer should not be difficult to find since we are all made to think that way; however, I am extremely baffled at the thought that this has gone on for many years without anyone making a bold move to question its sincerity and help create a debate. I can clearly disagree with this general depiction of the African continent, especially in the sub-Sahara region and in Ghana, where I was born and raised. It certainly was not so, though I recognize some similarities to some of the pictures and images of "Africa" that have been presented over the years.

There were schools and many educational institutions where a great number of us went to study and got our basic education to read and write, and I am proud to say that it is still so. I can almost picture that some might argue that my presentation might easily be a unique one, 'one in a million', most would say but it actually is not so. As far as I remember, my situation was not that different from a lot more from other families who did choose similar paths for their kids, as it is in many other societies around the world where differences in the status and levels of societies are utilized in many ways, be it good or bad, depending on how one sees it.

I enrolled in an international boarding school, and so were many of my age group and friends. There were many other playmates of mine who were alternatively attending the ordinary public school systems, and the only reason I can find is most probably because my guardians could afford the extra costs connected with the tuition and boarding setups of the international and boarding school educational systems of that time. Yes, there were distinctive differences between the poor and the rich, as is in many societies the world over, and though the gap between the rich and the poor has been dramatically altered over years, there are still a vast majority of people "living well" enough not to directly consider the entire continent "hell".

In some of my numerous discussions and arguments on this subject with many in the developed countries through which I try to debunk what I mostly consider are both the deliberate as well as the in deliberate efforts made to maintain and build this negative image of Africa. The most logical conclusion must be the admittance of ignorance being the underlying factor for their pre-supposition and conclusions.

Let's face it, it is rather easy to be ignorant about something that one knows little about, but in the case of Africa, though a greater number of people on this earth have little or no clue regarding the continent and its people, their way of lives, their characteristics, habits, their differences and similarities, I will bet it is the most widely opinionated subject of any other subject on earth. Everyone, anyone, anywhere, has an opinion on Africa and it makes me wonder where the various academicians from the various countries on this vast continent are, and there are many. Why not come to the defense of what I have always referred to as 'the most vulnerable society on earth'? Why? Simply because throughout history it has been told and shown to be that, held bondage by its own cultural, linguistic, tribal, racial and political diversities. It was so at the time in history and even worse as at the present since there seems to be no form of any attempt by anyone to question these several factual, semi-factual, and mythical presentations of the continent and its people.

I have, since long, proclaimed that I have a theory as to why Africa has the image it has and to what extent this image serves a purpose for those who have the need for this very dark, sinister, pathetic and humanly un-dignifying image.

I wish to make myself clear, that my well-thought-of elaboration of the length with which ignorance plays a very paramount and significant role in the image created of Africa is not to the exclusion of non-Africans alone but lots of citizens from countries on the African continent contributes immensely as well.

In considering the great strides made in our time, especially with that of the modern day electronic gadgets in direct connection with the information technology, it worries me that the continent of Africa and its people, especially those from sub-Sahara African communities, still remain in the very dark shadows of history's discarded 'filth and tragedy'. It baffles me to know that with the easy access via the World Wide Web, and all the good and positives that come with it, people care less about acquiring a little knowledge of the African continent. Even in this 21st century, many people seem not to know about the African continent and its various independent countries, in its geographic sense. In this age of 'Facebook', 'Twitter', 'YouTube', and all the other social media forums which, for more or less, connect people from across the globe in literally minutes, if not seconds, and yet I can bet that very few would be in a position to tell about the common bond that relates Egypt to Zimbabwe or Botswana. Is it because people do not care?

I have often asked myself why the next man, the next door neighbor or the lady at the local sports center believes that the man from Congo, Uganda, Gambia and I, are one and the same "African", but the man from Tunisia, Morocco and the Boer lady from South Africa is not?

Are people just ignorant due to no fault of theirs or they just cannot be bothered…..?

I believe in my heart that ignorance can begin at an early age if one is not directed and assisted with the access to the right information. I remember so well years ago, I was part of the coaching team that took part in the annually organized summer-weekly football/soccer schools arrangements by the Danish Football Union (DBU) and my usual preference was to coach both boys and girl between the ages of 12 and 16, based on a personal agenda I had. This temporal summer occupation often led to some interesting dialog involving myself and some of the young football/soccer boys and girls.

I remember so well a particular question that I got asked often, season after season. As surprised as I was, I welcome the opportunity to enlighten the youth, who I believe lacks the necessary information they needed to set their curiosities in check, so I was always ready to answer the many questions that were put to me, and usually, went further with what I think is an all-important elaboration. I guess you are wondering as to what type of questions and remarks were put to me. Well, the most significant question that comes to mind was me being asked to speak African. This was a question I always felt kind of bothered by (with my initial explanations), so I adopted a counter-question as a response to this particular question, and usually responded by: 'Can you speak European to me?' - my deliberate and calculated reaction to what I had always perceived as disrespectful of anyone, especially the adults who, in my opinion, do nothing to at least impart the basic knowledge to the youth, but then again, how would they if they themselves do not make efforts to know.

I agree that I seize the opportunity to embark on an unintended crusade to try and enlighten the adults through my reactionary response to the youth. The response to my question is usually that of an irritation since it is, of course, a common knowledge, that there is no language specifically referred to as "European", why then is it more acceptable as well as welcoming for anyone – be it a child or an adult, to refer to several independent languages spoken on an entire continent by millions and millions of people, to refer to it as "African"?

My maternal origin is Asante or Ashanti, which is part of the ethnic group across West Africa having 'Akan' as a common language with different dialects and identified as 'Twi'.

In seriously pondering over the above explanation of what "an African" is, I realize that I am even more farther away from understanding the logic supporting such explanations, which I am sure is the universally accepted version of the meaning of Africa and African.

In direct comparison to what I believe to be the acknowledged definitions of other societies around the world and with the recollection of what was taught me at school, the geographic and demographic aspects have very significant roles in forming such conclusions. I have often wondered as to whether other societies around the world would accept being identified for so long based on the continents they are located on. Though I see no serious concerns in being generally referred to by the continent from which one's country is, I doubt whether that would be accepted as an identity to be referred to by. To be identified as an Argentinian, a Brazilian, a Peruvian, a Chilean or a Columbian, I am sure would be more welcoming than to be identified as a South American. An American or a Canadian would in the same context, most definitely welcome being referred to by their nationalities.

The same can be said about the Germans, English, Scottish, Danes, Swedes, Norwegians, French, Belgians, Spanish and Hungarians, instead of being referred to as Europeans just because their countries are located on the European continent. Japanese, Chinese, Indian, Pakistani, Malaysian, Indonesian and Filipino would likewise prefer such identification than being identified via their continent. It so understandable and obvious that despite being from the same continent, there are cultural, traditional and national differences, to say the least, which defines the societies, collectively and individually, even in situations of common linguistic bonds. It is important to mention the various factors (be it positive or negative) that have contributed exclusively to the original creation of such countries and societies along with their unique identities and for which they seemingly have been proud of. For many years, I have seriously wondered why it is not so for the independent countries and societies on the African continent.

Someone somewhere must have decided (as is shown by the English definition of "African" above) that unlike the other nations on various continents around the world, people originating from the continent of Africa must have an identification reflective of their skin colors rather than that used in determining the identities of other countries elsewhere.

Would it (per definition and meaning given by the English dictionary as shown above) be an acceptable perception and belief around the world that an Egyptian, a Tunisian, a Moroccan or a Libyan is an African? Would

113

it be an acceptable perception for people from the African continent on this same subject? Would this perception and belief even be considered by the Egyptian, Tunisian, Moroccan, and the Libyan? What about the Indian, Arab, and European light-skin complexion citizens of countries in eastern and southern parts of the African continent whose origins are deeply rooted in the earlier generations who migrated and settled there some centuries ago?

This I believe is an interesting thought and question worth debating on.

Going by the definitions as given above in the English dictionaries, it should not be much of a puzzle, however, I am deeply confused and in a split situation, as to the real meaning and origin of the name Africa.

In my research to find an answer to this question that has puzzled me for so long, I read several kinds of literature from different sources dating as far back as in the early 'Ads'. One of the accessible information is that a historian by the name of Leo Africanus (1495-1554) attributed the origin of the name "Africa" to the Greek word 'phrike' (meaning 'cold and horror'), combined with a negative prefix a-, *so meaning a land of horror, and free of cold* - but the change of sound from 'ph' to 'f' in Greek is datable to about the 1st century, so this cannot be the origin of the name.

The name Africa came into western use through the Romans, who used the name 'Africa terra' – '*land of the Afri*' - plural, or '*Afer*' singular – for the Northern part of the continent, as the province of Africa with its capital in Carthage, corresponding to modern-day Tunisia on the African continent.

The origin of 'Afer' may either come from:

- The Phoenician 'afar' - dust;

- The 'Afri', a tribe – possibly Berber – who dwelt in North Africa in the Carthage area;

- The Greek word 'aphrike', meaning without cold;

- Or the Latin word "Africa", meaning sunny.

In a deep reflection of the above being an indication of the origin and meaning of the name Africa, I get filled with a vehement desire to unravel the complexity surrounding the name. Ironically, the name Africa is that given by those who will be considered 'non-Africans' and having little or no affiliation to the people to whom this reference is made. As much as I have been struggling with the unpleasant feeling of visiting the history of the African continent and its various citizens in all diversities, I am obliged to touch on some very sensitive factors in order to try and unravel what I refer to as the puzzle surrounding the name – "Africa".

As some will, while others might or might not agree, two events that have made their undisputed marks in history are 'The Slave Trade' and 'The colonization of sub-Sahara Africa', especially for someone like me with direct roots in Ghana – a country on the African continent.

As different historical facts have indicated, the transatlantic slave trade between the Americas and sub-Saharan Africa between the period 1500 – 1860, as well as the colonization of sub-Saharan Africa by primarily Western Europeans from the 1870s – 1900s, has without doubt, a direct reflection on how the words "Africa" and Africans were perceived then and very much so, now!

In what I sometimes refer to as my twisted imagination of humanity in general, I have no doubt that the given name "Africa" must clearly underline a defining factor in the "justification" with which the Africa and Africans then, were viewed as, and treated. Could there be a platform for discussions relating to the introduction of the word African, being considered inferior or less of a human being, directly relating to why a collective identification of a particular group of people, though with separate and diverse religions, cultures and traditions, has to be established, with apparent success?

Often times, I ask myself whether there are substantive reasons for my concerns regarding the seemingly harmless names referring to people collectively. My answer is, of course, yes, there are.

For reasons unknown and un-discussed (in my memory), the names Africa and Africans are seldom associated with positivity. Generalization is the order of time in memory, making it easier for the whole people to 'suffer' for the glaring ignorance of a majority. The expression: 'suffer' used in this context, embodies a number of reactions towards the 'defenseless' people on the African continent – south of the Sahara; chaffed, mocked, ridiculed, disrespected, looked down on, discriminated upon, chastised, mistreated, inhumanely treated and a whole bunch of negative narratives.

The words "Africa" or "Africans" are so loosely used but often without really understanding what it means but for the common perception of that of a person, with a type of physical features, and coming from the continent of Africa – south of the Sahara. As pointed out above, this could not be so wrong, except that the source of such words and meaning, had some form of prejudicial agendas, associated with them.

116

In this 21st century of this computer-age and the vast technological development available to us, and with so many learning tools accessible to us, it angers and frustrates me when a great majority of people still refer to a place and people of such wide diversities, with one word (name).

The frequent use of the word "Africa" in not only referring to a place, but also as a common denominator for a continent of over 50 independent countries with a combined population of over 1.2 billion, over a thousand languages, different and multiple cultures, diverse social structures and foundations, is simply absurd. It is the only place on this planet where such blunder is cynically embraced.

"Africa" and "African", is often used when people do not know the true identity of the country or person in question. The common reference - "African" is often a substitution for the identity of dark-skin people from communities in sub-Saharan Africa. This might be that people either do not care or could not be bothered about the true identity of the person in question, as long as the individual is dark-skinned and originating from a country in sub-Saharan Africa.

Chapter 9
The Mentalities

I have of late been intensively discussing the possibility of spending my Christmas holiday in my country of birth – Ghana, primarily due to my intent to get away from the increasing cold, dark, wet and depressing winter days in Northern Europe, into a warm and nice tropical weather and atmosphere.

I am, therefore, in constant telephone communication with my relatives down in Ghana, however, I sense the tone of caution I am getting from them regarding my intended arrival date. I am being cautioned and advised to postpone my arrival date to a date after December 7. The significance of December 7, 2012, in this context, is that the general elections to vote a new president into the office to rule the country for the following term are taking place.

'Please, do not come down until after the elections are held,' I am being told so my obvious question is, of course, to be given the reason why such advice. With so much sincerity, care and concern from almost all I have been speaking to, the fear of an outbreak of intense upheaval, disruption and chaos in their society from the aftermath of the voting. I have tried to discuss and debate this seemingly radical viewpoint with them, stressing on

118

the fact that it is simply ridiculous to me (from my base in a European capital city) that they can have such presumption of an important and significant democratic event in their lives. I would think that any of such concerns and worries must be the farthest in the minds of any human being with the intent of embracing true democracy but who am I to question and judge them, or anyone for that matter?

Dancing, dancing in one form or the other, in various local traditional presentations across the tribal societies of almost all the African countries, is an almost too familiar site. Dancing, in almost all of its forms, is perceived in all other societies across the globe as an indication of happiness and joyous times. In welcoming others of important significance from both inside and from outside their societies, we have often seen and witnessed, notable on TV and in films, of how the traditional dances of all forms are displayed. This, I have made note of, is the same with all the various African societies, no matter their ethnicity, color and race. One would wonder why the mention of this, well, because I wonder as to whether or not dancing, as much as we know it to be, really depicts the happiness and joy that we know it brings to the dancer.

The point in my mentioning all of the above is to hopefully get the view of others on this subject among many others that I have been wondering about, and has been 'eating me up'. I am also filled with the hope of finding some reasonable answers to this particular question I frequently ask myself: 'If dancing (in the forms we know it to be) is an expression on the outside of one´s inner joy, then why are my African people always showing that we know to be the opposite?'

I once lived in an affluent part of a European country capital and as it is with all other cities in the world, living in such areas do come with its price; the high cost of living. These apartment buildings were newly constructed and having a twist of very modern architecture. I would say these apartment blocks were differently structured in very fine tune with the landscape, both on which the apartment blocks stood and that of the adjoining buildings nearby. As little a knowledge I have on architecture, my admiration for beautifully constructed pieces of work did indeed get tested and I fell in love with these apartments, leading consequently to my moving into one of them.

It was the first time for me experiencing the beautiful artwork of a combination of solid concrete materials, some in the round, semi-round shapes and others in square shapes and carefully "tailored" grass and hedges leaving a very fresh lively green and gray color combination.

There was a sense of pride I felt living in such an apartment, notwithstanding the high rental cost, even in those days, but was gladly paying, for the pleasure.

The wife of an acquaintance of mine, both from Ghana, had on one of their periodic visits to me mentioned her intention to "lend" my apartment and its surroundings to be photographed in. My initial reaction to her request was that of 'no problems, anytime'. After a short while, my curiosity kicked in and prompted into me asking her as to the reason for her request made, and her answer actually did not surprise me; it must have been due probably, to me considering myself, an "African".

'Why would she make such a request, should there be any difference in the location of choice for being photographed?' I am sure these questions come to your minds as well and rightfully so.

'Could there be any reasonable arguments for such a request?' Many would ask. Well, I did for a number of years wonder about why 'we' can have such modes of thinking.

Christine and her husband lived in a then low-income-housing area of the city. This area did not enjoy the best of reputations as it is close to 'the red-light district' of the city, where the porn cinemas and shops are located, and plus, it being the main base for the city's prostitutes. This area was and is still considered an area mostly inhabited by low-income workers and was somehow a bit 'run down' in comparison to a greater part of the city. I must quickly add though that this same area, including its central part, has in the last few several years undergone drastic renovations which were undertaken by the authorities of the city's municipality, resulting in a total transformation into being one of the most modern and 'chic' areas of the city, with cafés, restaurants and shops.

Sunday noon, and as agreed, Christine and husband came into my apartment carrying all the items needed for the shoot. Knowing 'our people', I was not a bit surprised in my thinking of why they had to carry all those extra clothing, shoes, and accessories with them when they both looked well-dressed having been to church earlier. We went about the various duties of helping Christine go through her multiple changes for the various photo shots taken in different postures and backgrounds. Not being a bit impressed by the whole event of that afternoon, I went into a thinking mode after they had left, to find answers to the questions raised earlier, in relation to why this should take place in my neighborhood; something I am sure you must also be doing, reading this.

Not in the least making any effort to impose my thinking on others, I can allow myself to guess, as I did not engage Christine or her husband in any attempt to ask for reasons why. I do not believe it was necessary since I am myself a product of this mindset. For very good and plausible reasons so well known to us and discussed in other chapters in this book, it is a mindset that allows us to make every effort, be it consciously or sub-consciously, NOT to present the 'bad' and the 'negative' sides of the 'developed countries' to our people back in our home countries. Ironically, this is exactly what is done to the "African" and the "African" societies back on the continent of Africa, and, to the rest of the world..

Both myself, Christine and a whole others would rather make an effort to convey to our friends and families back home, the way we have been "programmed" to think, that everything in Europe, in North America and the rest of the world, apart from in sub-Saharan African societies are the finest and better than our own. That we, 'the Africans', are privileged to be living in these fine and 'near perfect' societies. We – 'the Africans', even make extra efforts to hide the 'nasty sides' in the developed countries, thereby re-enforcing the belief in us that is already cemented in our minds for centuries back, that life is good, cozy and perfect in the developed countries and everywhere else than in Africa; in sub-Saharan Africa.

It was and still is today quite common to see photos of people from countries in sub-Sahara Africa who have traveled abroad to other parts of the world (especially in the so-called developed countries) either as students or for other reasons in various 'happy-go-lucky' postures, surroundings, and smiling faces in partying-atmospheres, despite the disrespect and lack of human dignity they are very often subjected to.

Without exception, the dark-skin people from countries in sub-Saharan Africa like to show through the photos they send back to their families back home a depiction of wealth, riches and good-living of their host countries, despite the flaws they experience thereof.

Photos showing nice and expensive cars, push houses, wealthy neighborhoods, partying, smiles, and more positive atmosphere; depictions they will not present from their own societies back in their home countries. There are equally bad and negative depictions of their host countries, so why would they rather choose to show the more positive sides? This is a question that has baffled me for a long time. Is it because we have been made to think less of ourselves and more positive of those outside the sub-Saharan region of the Africa continent?

The thinking process of many from the societies in sub-Saharan Africa is that their whole existence is directly connected to what the Europeans, Americans, and the outside world does, thinks and decides, and 'why would it not be so?' I often ask myself. Generations in the various communities across sub-Saharan Africa have experienced nothing other than being 'fed', 'led', 'guided' and saved, time and time again by the white man (which is a common reference to the international community), so I can understand this way of thinking and perception. Perception being a reality for many, it is fair to conclude that for a great majority of dark-skin people in communities in sub-Saharan Africa, this is their reality. This reality, as understandable as it is, creates a very serious downside for the entire societies in sub-Saharan Africa, affecting them negatively in every way.

If one's whole existence is dependent on Aid and Assistance from sources other than your own, the automatic reaction, in my opinion, can be that of NOT being innovative, productive and active, to provide for yourself and as stated elsewhere in this book, such mindset must be very beneficial to those who have the intent to exploit the people, and all that comes with it.

'Why should I struggle to provide for myself and my family when the provisions can be made available to me?' I am sure is a thought commonly crossing the minds of some of the dark-skin peoples in sub-Saharan Africa, without them realizing the negative consequences it comes to bear on them, or could it simply be, that some just do not care? These conclusions of mine are based partly on the personal experiences I have had through direct personal interactions and conversations with people from these parts of the world, and from my own suppositions as well.

I dare conclude that the eventual thinking of a vast majority of dark-skin people in communities across sub-Saharan Africa is a direct contributor to the obvious decadence in the various societies down there. This is true to the extent by which the communities have become dependent on help and assistance from other sources than their own, making them dependent, unproductive, lazy, and un-innovative to their own cause.

What I classify as being strange is the common belief that seems to exist, that everything good comes from 'the white man' and the societies outside of their own, making them ignore the good and the abundant resources that are within their own communities, which is obviously exploited by those outside and sadly, some from inside, with conspicuous pre-intentions.

Even to this day, to travel out from the sub-Sahara African communities to Europe, the Americas and elsewhere, is in the minds of a lot of people, something special in itself, just as can be attributed to the post-colonial era and the effects it had on people's thinking, having a direct association with the 'whites' either by being appointed and/or by subsequent choices, being considered as a privilege and consequently looked up to, by a majority in the communities.

Instead of confronting the problems in the communities, tackling them and finding solutions, the various communities seem to choose the path of receiving from donors from abroad and ignore the vast rich resources available to them, and plus, their rightful demands to their leaders to be responsible and accountable, in my opinion. The responsibilities for the well-being of the citizens from various communities down in sub-Saharan Africa seems to have been wrongly misplaced, leaving room for continuous decadence in the societies they live in.

Chapter 10
Effect and ID

I have noticed that anytime I pay a visit to Ghana, I get this very confused bitter-sweet feeling which I am as yet, able to dissect and confront. I probably like the passive feeling I experience within me.

'Why this bitter-sweet feeling?' one might ask. Bitter because I usually experience upon entering the arrival and immigration hall, that this very strong emotional feeling from the excitement of coming back home, plus, the internal built-up anxiety and hype from thinking about the 'privileged' position one must be in. This is no fluke, and many can identify with this scenario. When traveling for a visit home, and though I dislike generalizing, I would dare say that all who hail from an African country would recognize this feeling of being in one way or the other, a sense of being superior.

I would very much like to visit this topic; the generalization of Africa being acceptable and willingly applied by all (both domestic and foreign), apparently to all humans and things directly from, and connected with, the dark-skin population from the African continent.

I have often wondered as to the source of the term and reference; "African", being a black person from the African continent.   Not that it is in any way offensive to me, but I have often wondered as to whether it was a conscious effort on someone's part to attain such outcome. Allow me the time to express my concerns. As I recall, when Ghana (then Gold Coast) achieved their independence from the British in 1957, the then leader of the political movement – Dr. Kwame Nkrumah gave a significant speech on that evening, amongst which this was, quote:

'The independence of Ghana is meaningless, unless it is linked up with the total liberation of the African continent,' unquote.

What did he mean by such words? And in my own confused mind, what bearing it had, and has had on the subject I am trying to elaborate in the coming pages?

I have hardly heard anywhere, from anyone, on any subject involving one or more nations on the African continent, without making direct reference to the collective term of "in Africa". Why do we not hear similar references from dealings and issues with South American nations, or Asian, Southeast Asian nations, European nations, etc.? All these geographical regions comprise of independent and sovereign nations, just as the continent of Africa does and yet, I do not recollect specific references to any particular nation in a collective way, as does the continent of Africa. My question, therefore, is why?

I am born in Ghana, a sovereign and independent nation on the West coast of Africa, surrounded by other sovereign and independent nations, but how sovereign and independent are all these nations in the real sense of the word 'independent', regarding its daily references in terms of the politics, social, religious and cultural independence, to the average person?

It beats my mind to think that a Chinese would make reference to a Korean and conclude 'We, Northeast Asians', or an Indian referring in the same way to a Pakistani as 'We, Asians'. Neither would a British person refer to a Polish or a Spanish person as 'We, Europeans'.

This is, in my opinion, due to the simple fact that their geographic positions do not necessarily make them one people and neither do their color and common preferences. Their respective political and geographical sovereignty is widely embodied in their cultural, ethnic, religious and diversified independence, which remains that way to themselves and the world. Why then, is it that it is very common to hear references to the term "in Africa", made continuously by people, including those from the African continent (when referring to issues relating to independent nations and people), be they illiterates or academicians? What is really African, and who is really African?

March 6 is a date I am very familiar with. It is this date way back in 1957 that Ghana got its independence from Great Britain, and as expected, is celebrated annually by Ghanaians and friends of Ghana around the world. 1957….it's so many years ago since the struggles for independence from colonial rule by the leaders ended however, it has crossed my mind so many times as to where this so called independence is practiced and enjoyed.

In reality, yes, the country has been free to rule and govern itself, has been free to take decisions relating to the growth and progress of the nation and her citizens as a whole. This, I believe, is the same for all the other independent nations on the African continent. Acknowledging all this and still puzzled by the independent identities of all these nations, be it good or bad.

As I have mentioned in other parts of this book, I personally feel that it is very vital that the independence of each nation on the African continent be recognized and upheld, both internally, and externally as well, to enhance the development and well-being of the citizens of these nations. As much as many might disagree with me, I hope that some few will come to the realization that with the very common reference of Africa being a collective name widely used, its people from the various countries have no identities.

Many may argue as to the importance of having the various independent countries being referred to by their names, and whether it makes a difference (especially to people from outside the continent).

I might very much be in the minority, but I do strongly believe that in referring to independent nations, it is only proper for their rightful names to be acknowledged. My personal reason and concerns are that in the omission of a direct identity reference, lots of injustice is done to the various nations and her people – especially in the case of the nations on the African continent. As I have often wondered, why is there so little known of the various independent nations on the African continent? As mentioned, I have wondered why it is openly acceptable not to refer to an independent nation by its name, instead of the name of the continent on which it is located. It is indeed the case with all other independent nations worldwide.

Following are some of the examples I am referring to: Sri Lanka and a dish from Sri Lanka, Brazil and Brazilian soccer/football, Vietnam and the Vietnam War, Colombia and Colombian coffee, Mexico, Germany, Japan, The Philippines, India, Pakistan, Iran, Saudi Arabia, Indonesia, I could go on and on, with many examples and what all this means, is the recognition of these nations and societies by identifying them by their rightful names. My deepest concern is that the identities of almost all the independent 50 plus independent nations on the African continent, except a few – notably the Northern Arabic-culture-dominated countries and the Republic of South Africa, are seldom used.

It is rather 'proper' for many (ironically including people from the African continent) to generalize in reference to any instance involving an African country, or someone from (especially) the dark-skin dominated regions. I am inclined to conclude that this might be borne out of ignorance, as is often agreed when I have debated on this subject and yet, why has this form of ignorance not been replaced by the 'wind of knowledge gracefully blowing across our planet' in this 21st century? It seems to me to be an unimportant subject to many, but I must say that if truly thought about, this has a direct or indirect impact on the view of the African continent, its development and existence. How and why? Many might ask.

You might agree with me that the name "Africa" is synonymous with everything negative; therefore, the identity of the "African" is also automatically synonymous with everything negative. This is very detrimental to the development of the societies and the citizens of these various independent nations on the African continent.

I saw an advertisement on CNN the other day for the promotion of a product and interestingly, it started by stating that every country has its unique identity. This is so true, or rather; it is supposed to be so, however, can you conclude the same about the dark-skin dominated nations on the African continent? I personally do not think so.

I have had reactions from some people who have heard me express such concerns about what I refer to as true identities of various citizens of various African countries, which is more of why I make so much of this subject. Many have said to me that they have (as long as they remember) always been made to think that the reference of "an African" is to identify a specific person with some significant features and what that is, is anybody's guess. After a purposeful voluntary keen observation of the societies in the 'developed countries' and around the world, their views and perceptions of other societies other than their own, I reluctantly conclude that the societies of the various dark-skin-populated countries on the African continent have either lost their identities, or have never been recognized.

The best meaningful explanation that I have been given is ignorance. The ignorance displayed by the societies outside of the African continent and most certainly and surprisingly, from the communities within the African continent as well.

'It's because we do not know of any other condition or situation other than what we are being shown on TV, or hear on the radio,' this is usually the honest response I get from a lot of people in Europe. My very serious concern is, why? Why has this been so for all these years without any effort on anyone's part to 'do right?'

By 'do right', I am referring to why has this been accepted and tolerated for so long. So long, that it has become part of the thinking and perception of the majority.

Recently, in one of the local TV news bulletin, it was read out that the police in Copenhagen were seriously looking for a male offender of the law whose description could only be given as having an "African" appearance. I called the TV station to ask about their meaning of 'an African appearance', and they suggested that I make contact with the police as the message was delivered on TV as a request from the police, which I did. My prompt follow-up call to the main police head Office telephone got me to talk to an officer whose response to the same question I had asked the TV station a short while earlier, was that of serious agitation and frustration at my seemingly unnecessary concern and question.

In one of the early morning cookery shows on one of the Danish TV stations, a known Danish cook was preparing 'an African dish'. This cook had apparently arrived back home from a trip he had made to the nation of Tanzania in East Africa and was keen on presenting a dish from Tanzania, however, he (unsurprisingly) refers to his art of cooking as being an 'African dish'. Why, why call such a dish an African dish? Why not call it a Tanzanian dish when in similar instances, the dish in question would be referred to by the place, society or nation from where the raw materials or ingredients are from? Why would the same cook appear in similar situations and refer to his cookery by the name of the society from where the ingredients and art are from? One may ask. Many numerous examples we are too familiar with – 'French cuisine', 'Spanish, Italian or German delicacy', 'English cookery', and 'Australian wines'. As I am trying to point out with all these examples, there is a distinct identity trait directly connected with the society from where these foods and art come.

In my sporadic discussions and rather short debates with interested people, I often get the feeling of 'why do bother', or 'very complicated subject to comprehend', or the vague attempts to come with some meaning in the identity status that I am so into.

'Does it really matter?' is the usual feeling I get from most people. 'We have always known and referred to them as Africans and see nothing negative about it,' is also the verbal reaction I get from some people.

I have often wondered as to whether I am the only one in this whole world who thinks that the lack of 'identity' is crucial to the existence of any living thing, and in this case, the population from especially the sub-Sahara region of the African continent? I do not know! I have no answer to this question, however, my thorough observation over a long period has led me to conclude that it is okay with a great majority and that not only is it acceptable, it is very suitable.

As I have mentioned elsewhere in this book, when one hears the name Brazil, it should go without saying that majority of us easily identifies it with positivity;

brilliant soccer/football, Samba music and dance, making merry, joy sunshine, beaches, etc. Despite the problems and issues some of us have heard of with the nation of Cuba, do we not associate positivity with hearing the name, music, sports or world-renowned cigars, to mention some? The same can be said of Jamaica and many other small nations in the Caribbean and the West Indies. Argentina, Uruguay, Peru, Colombia, Mexico and Haiti are all, irrespective of their geographic location, identified by their names. These identifications (in my view) do contribute, be it positively or negatively, to the overall perception of the said country's reputation, which in turn immensely contributes to the images formed by the societies of this world and the effects their eventual decisions directly have.

The hard-fought independence achieved by many of the nations in sub-Saharan Africa through extensive and lengthy struggles from the colonial powers, is in my opinion, meaningless in terms of the diverse human and technological developments and what it has to offer.

Looking back from the early times at the wave of independent struggles in the mid-1950s that swept across the continent and the promise it brought with it for the millions of their citizens, and compared to that of the last 30 plus years, I can conclude that the expected positive developments for the majority of individuals are very few and far in between. There are those who have difficulties in agreeing with my argument emphasizing on the lack of identity as being one of the major factors amongst significant others, contributing to the stagnant and rather deteriorating state.

My point and argument is deeply embedded in the name "Africa".

Africa is the continent on which the various independent nations are located; therefore, the logic must be that people from these nations are Africans, just like it is with the European continent and Europeans, the South Americans from the South American continent, North Americans from the North American continent, etc. In summing up my argument, the seeming lack of the deserving identity for the people from the sub-Sahara African continent is seriously detrimental to the development of their citizens.

In my opinion, the common and acceptable practice of not identifying the various independent nations on the continent of Africa, especially those in the sub-Saharan regions, has dire consequences than one would care to know.

Because there is far too much generalization due to several factors including ignorance, lack of interest and superiority complex amongst others, which in turn has created a very negative image of the people, which in turn has become a barrier to success.

Denmark is separated from both Sweden and Norway by a body of water, and these independent countries form part of the collective reference as the Scandinavian countries. It takes less than 30 minutes to cross from Denmark into Sweden, and Sweden actually shares a common land border as well with Norway.

It is very easy to recognize the common trait amongst the societies and their people, in terms of their looks, their characteristics and even their languages and yet despite this commonality, their identities are always established. I am yet to witness, in any shape or form, a situation where despite the common traits amongst the Scandinavian countries, a reference to the identity of either a citizen or a particular country has been generalized. For example, when an incident takes place in any of these countries, the identity (be it Denmark, Sweden or Norway) will be mentioned and not by a general reference.

'There was a motor accident this morning on highway E40 this morning involving a Swedish car, and a Danish truck' or 'a Norwegian woman/man is wanted by the police for questioning', rather, 'A German boy', 'an American film', 'a Brazilian actor', 'a Chinese, a Japanese', etc., would be the usual info. I hardly ever hear any references via the names of their various continents, as in: 'An accident took place this morning involving two Scandinavians/Europeans', or 'a South American couple is wanted by the police for questioning'.

Are the rightly-earned identities of these societies and its people unimportant to the outside world? Why are some very established and high-profile-journalists, academicians (both in the developed and under-developed societies), astute TV and film personalities, and much more, constantly and comfortably generalizing when it has to do with sub-Sahara Africa? Is it deliberate, or are their acts based simply on not knowing, and if so, why not make efforts to learn?

After all, there is little excuse for a great majority of us. We had geography as part of the fundamentals of our academic learning process.

I have often times been irritated by the constant generalization in relating to the various independent countries and societies on the sub-Sahara African continent. 'Should it be that difficult to recognize the differences in the people and the society at large?' Are there reasons as to why it is so? I would often ask myself questions like: 'Are there any hidden agendas from faceless powers in control of the universe who are manipulating the situation?'

How can a very well respected British sports commentator in his commenting on a big sporting event like the Olympic Games, present athletes from predominantly East Africa and athletes from Northern Africa as having different origins? At a point during one of the Track and Field disciplines, he commented as follows: 'It is now heating up between the Africans and the Moroccans.' Through the learning in my school days, I was taught in the subject of Geography about the various countries making up the African continent and I know that Morocco is located on the continent of Africa. I just heard an advertisement on the radio for various sales on various products in a grocery store chain, for amongst others, "an African item" which is drastically reduced. In introducing the newlywed princess of Sweden, it was said that she is actively involved in an aid organization for African children when the reality is that her work is with children in South Africa.

I wonder if the same would and could be said in a similar situation involving other geographical parts of the world. Could the term 'European kids' be used when indeed the situation involves kids from specifically

Romania, Germany, Denmark, France or Bulgaria? The answer is a definite no!

These few examples amongst many leads back to my question asked in an earlier segment as to why it is so. It feels almost automatic for the international community to refer to various countries with their true identities via their names except for those in sub-Sahara Africa. What surprises me though is that this practice is not excluded only to those outside the sub-Sahara regions of Africa but also many within.

My very serious concern, position, and conclusion for the omission (either consciously or subconsciously) are what I consider as very detrimental to the eventual development and existence of sub-Saharan Africa and its citizens.

It is no secret that the name "Africa" is, without a doubt, connected with everything negative and thereby, linking "an African" to the same traits of negativity.

In my efforts to find out the origin as well as the reason for the act of generalizing "Africa & Africans", I can conclude without a doubt, that it must have everything to do with their race and ethnicity. I am sure there are many that might disagree with me, but then I would wish they will be able to help me understand why a Tunisian, Egyptian, Moroccan, Algerian or Libyan from Northern African region would be referred to by the name of their nations and commonly referred to as Arabs, which must be due to their ethnicity. Why should they not be referred to as Africans when their countries are located on the African continent? Is this not so?

Citizens from various countries on the continents other than the African represent the norms and cultures of

138

their individual societies and countries and not their continents. I strongly believe this should be the same too for the citizens and countries of sub-Saharan Africa.

Is an Egyptian an African? How about a Tunisian or a Moroccan? I have periodically had such discussions with some people of all ethnicity and as expected, the responses and reactions have been different however, the fact of the inability to comprehend my concern of the lack of identity for the individual countries in sub-Saharan Africa is so clear.

This is why I conclude that the choice (consciously or unconsciously) to refer to the countries and people of sub-Saharan Africa has everything to do with the color of the skin, much more than their general characters.

It is interesting to me that in my efforts to find the reason to the subject above, making reference to the color of the skin as being the underlining factor in the collective identification of a group of people is even more significant when other black people from places outside the African continent, e.g. from USA, England, Caribbean, etc. do use the term "Africa" and "Africans", however, more in tune with the different dialects of the English, French and Portuguese languages (introduced by the colonial authorities many years back) spoken. The various ethnic languages are also helpful in the identification of the African.

I remember so well of some significant incidents years ago during some of my time as a soccer/football coach for young boys of the ages between 12 and 16 years in Denmark, when some dared ask me whether I spoke African.

As much as I often was surprised and even felt insulted sometimes at such blatant ignorance, I equally understood their innocent curiosity and how it was no fault of theirs but rather that of their parents, guardians and teachers. I often reacted a bit harsh, in my efforts to respond and try to enlighten them, by asking them whether they spoke 'European'. As young as I considered them to be, I usually felt some form of surprise on their parts relating to my question, as if to indicate to me how I could not know that being Danish by birth, they spoke Danish and that there was no language called 'European'.

I always seized the opportunity to combat this form of ignorance, especially among the youth, by carefully try explaining the right information to them.

The reference to the continent of Africa being 'The dark continent', must add some strength to my position as laid out in this chapter. But then again, this must be a reference directed at the sub-Sahara region. There are many Caucasians who are born and bred in some African countries – especially in the Southern region. In the Republic of South Africa and Zimbabwe, to mention a few, have many citizens of Caucasian ethnicity and I wonder how they will be referred to by people outside their countries of origin.

The immediate above brings my mind to my own family from Ghana. One of my female cousins was adopted at infancy by my Auntie and her husband from a European country. My cousin, who is of mixed race and who by exterior body features, is much lighter in her skin complexion by looks. Several years later, she is happily married and settled in England with her English husband

and kids and I must remember to add that she is currently a British citizen and has been for a great number of years.

She told me of an interesting incident that took place at one of their extended family gatherings, when she reacted apparently to an unpleasant comment by a family member about Ghana. Her sudden reaction in defense of Ghana, her adoptive country and a citizen of (by virtue of her parents and intent), caused a counter-reaction and comment by this same family member.

'Strange,' she said, as to why my cousin should even have the need to react to such comments about Ghana...

'Why she should be concerned and bothered about a comment made about a distant country she is not from.'

'I cannot stand idly by when such comments are being made about Ghana, I am Ghanaian, remember that,' are the comments my cousin made in reacting to the family member. 'Wow'! Was my silent reaction to how she could think in such a way. Her features, her thinking and her ways of seeing and doing things are so English. Her current life's foundation is, and has been for so many years, grounded in the English way so how can she even "think Ghanaian", as well as sympathize with Ghana. Can she be considered an "African"?

As a summary on this subject, I believe that for whatever reason in displaying and enforcing the ignorance by people, on the lack of reference to both the countries and their citizens by their true identities, it is seriously contributing in the most negative way to the development of the independent countries and their citizens on the continent of Africa, south of the Sahara.

Chapter 11
Superiority and Inferiority Complexes

'Africanized-Bees', what is that? 'Are there also some other living organisms that have been categorized under the name "Africa"?' I have been asking myself. It seems like anything with a connection to the 'terminology' – "Africa", is negative or bad.

'Countries we usually compare ourselves with,' I have heard this sentence being mentioned often by some TV and radio anchormen and anchorwomen and in the public forum as well.

'What really should this mean?' I have often wondered. 'There must be a reason why lots of efforts are made and being made to intensify, in my opinion, this sense of classification and categorization of human beings.' My hope is to be able to dissect some challenging theories I have struggled with in my efforts to try to find some form and understanding to this puzzle later in this chapter.

Listening to commentaries from sports commentators around the world, specifically in soccer/football – is one area with a wide display of an attitude I refer to as "superiority complex" on the part of most non-Africans. In 1992, for the very first time, the bi-annual football/soccer tournament for the ultimate championship title amongst all the African independent nations was televised live to international viewers outside the continent of Africa by the TV station – 'SCREEN SPORT,' which was of English language orientation. The tournament, as mentioned, was beamed live from the West African country of Senegal. It was rather a historic event and up until this day, I have often wondered what 'the catch' was for Screen Sport. Screen Sport was later taken over in some sort of a merger with the current 'EUROSPORT,' who continues televising this event every 2nd year.

Historically, this event had not been shown any form of interest in the past by the world outside of the African continent. This historic development had without a doubt, a possibility to showcase to football/soccer lovers from outside of the African Continent a very positive side of a sporting event that we have loved and followed for so long, so those of us with interest were filled with content for this surprise 'gift'. It was new I must say. So very little was thought of in terms of the wide interest one had hoped for. Remember, the only source of information about football/soccer played on the African continent had always been that shown during the FIFA World football/soccer championship which takes place every four years.

'Fast forward' to the following years after which, as mentioned, is still televised by EUROSPORT but based on individual country's independent commentaries. I do remember the particular observation I had made by the then sole English commentator by the name of Archie McPherson and his rather unfamiliar way of giving commentaries on the games. It was interesting to hear some of the comments he used in reference to the various players, using the pronoun – 'they' in referring to the players. As innocent as this might appear to be, my concern for this remark made by this commentator is, why I do not hear a similar reference to players playing in Europe, South America and elsewhere. It is like him making reference to creatures from out of space, from Mars or something to that effect.

In my careful efforts to try walking a fine line between the direct references of slavery, pre-colonial and pro-colonial societies on the African continent as the basis for some of my observations and comments, I have no choice but to periodically bring up some of these significant historical incidents to support my conclusions.

The tendency to either feel less of a human, or to be made to feel less of a human, is an experience I am sure many people have had in one form or the other, however, "inferiority complex" is a widely used reference in many situations in our daily lives, through subjective recognition of a kind or the other, but not the opposite term: 'superiority complex'.

I have in my quest to find the meaning to why in many instances, dark-skinned people from the African countries south of the Sahara are widely seen differently compared to others, and in most extreme instances, made to feel inferior.

As mentioned earlier in trying to avoid making this look like a typical racist-tone issue, it is important to point out that it is also a fact in many instances where such attitudes have surprisingly been exhibited by other black people of different orientation.

144

A day, a week or a month does not go by without an image depicting the sorry sight of what we all can conclude to be "Africa and Africans". One does not need any thorough understanding or observation to come to terms with this reality of our world.

In Denmark, as well as in many other countries outside the continent of Africa, are several humanitarian relief organizations with seemingly one purpose and goal, which is in more ways than one, to come to the aid of Africa in various forms in the need for emergency help and assistance. 'Boernefonden/Children Fund', 'Unicef', 'Redbarnet/Save the Children', 'Roed Kors/Red Cross', 'SOS Boernebyerne/SOS Children Villages', 'Planfadder/Plan Sponsorship', to mention a very few of the countless established relief organizations in Denmark alone.

One might wonder as to why I am raising this subject in relation to the above headline in this section. The answer is simply, my questioning of the various messages relating to these campaigns for aid and assistance and the effects (be it positive or negative) it has on the societies around the world.

I personally have an issue with the various images depicted in the campaigns run constantly in the media by the humanitarian organizations and have contacted them on a number of occasions to express my concerns. My main worry is what I have noticed for a great number of years in all the campaigns, and non-exclusive to the other, which I consider is the very essence of these campaigns – to attain pity!

A number of years ago, I was contacted by 'a concerned man' who had seen a feature in the Danish national TV news bulletin on a subject he knew was very dear to my heart and wanted me to see.

I was late in catching the segment of the news bulletin he wanted me to see so I called the TV station and requested to know more about this feature, who further directed me to the journalist behind this feature. I did, eventually, get hold of a duo of journalists who had an insight into the various activities of some of the prominent humanitarian organizations in Africa and especially, the very strange and suspect behaviors of their workers in expediting their duties. Apparently, it had been documented that most of the aid workers who had been transferred to various postings in various countries in Africa had been more on vacation than expediting their duties to which they were assigned. 'On vacation'! Yes, spending most of their days relaxing at the poolside at their various luxury hotels, enjoying the services and all that comes with the regular luxury vacation one can imagine and plus, the familiar fun and parties with the locals in the bars and nightclubs.

This claim by the journalists had triggered a debate that was to take place in one of the studios of the TV stations, and the main topic was, amongst the elaboration of this claim, the obvious position apparently taken by the representatives of some of the humanitarian organizations – the defense of such claim. I got a call from the TV station and was subsequently invited to the studio along with the journalists whose efforts had contributed to such conclusion, to be part of a nationwide televised TV studio debate. My role had been agreed in advance and that was to highlight what I have noticed, and tried in some ways to inform some of the

146

organizations through the several telephone calls I make to them concerning the 'usual' contents in their campaigns, and the often distorted messages in their quest to gain pity with the public, which can be demeaning and inhuman.

There is a saying I have often heard in America which goes like this: 'To win, somebody has to lose', and in many situations when I come across the many campaign images by the humanitarian organization via the media, I cannot help myself but conclude as to whether a great number of those images, are indeed a reflection of the 'goal' (I am sure) set. I am often concerned as to the message some of these campaigns carry, and I can conclude that the pathetic images are still being shown and in some cases, even more demeaning, as if the undertone of these messages is that, the rougher the images, the more the pitiful effect will come to bear on the recipients of these messages.

The few times I have succeeded in engaging in a rather short dialogue between myself and some of these relief organizations in my efforts to outline this point of the demeaning images they present, I have been met with all sorts of explanations which I see as defensive, evasive, and sometimes nonchalant. In my last telephone conversation with one of these organizations when I tried bringing to the attention of their representatives that I was talking to, he did concur to my point raised, however, he insisted and tried to make me understand that it does become necessary, in their opinion, to take that route if they are to succeed in reaching their goal. What this meant and means is that "the end justifies the means", which is extremely repulsive to me as a human being.

Being derogative of other human beings just to achieve their goal has a very long lasting negative effect on both the giving end, and the receiving end, without it being that obvious.

How long can one have pity, or is expected and required to have pity?

I ask this because if I am right about the intent of the organizations in their efforts to achieve their goals, then there should be concerns as to whether those goals set would be attained considering the seemingly dwindling interest to donate to the public at large.

'How do I come to such conclusion and how do I know this for a fact?' I have been asked on some occasions. Well, it's obvious to me that the interest in donating to the causes being exhibited time and time again in the media, significantly in the past decade when asked, has drastically diminished in comparison to what it was before, due to many reasons as mentioned above or similar. Even in times where having pity for fellow human beings in dire needs become automatic, the foundation for giving assistance or help to those in need should bear the fruit and not be seen as being in a stagnant state. The latter is precisely what I fear the very calculated campaigns by the organizations will lead to.

The conscious and sub-conscious notions of being more of a human being than the next person due arguably to visible circumstances prevailing in our everyday lives and flaunting it, to the detriment of others, is what I refer to as having a "superiority complex". The opposite conscious and sub-conscious notions of being less of a human being due arguably to unfavorable conditions, either by internal and external circumstances and choices, are what I would refer to as having a complex of being inferior to others.

I am following a documentary being shown on one of the Danish TV channels as of now, concerning the alleged unfair practices by the huge cocoa and chocolate business conglomerate on the farmers and producers, especially in West Africa. Mr. Miki Mistrati, the presenter of this program, is an established Danish journalist who was following up on his earlier attempt to try and uncover these alleged malpractices, including the wide use of child labor. I commend Mr. Mistrati and his team for a wonderful work done, however, my focus is mainly on the inter-human aspect of this documentary.

It is appalling to me seeing the clear disregard for basic respect and lack of decency for another human being. It might look like the obvious. State of things might come about, in terms of the cause-and-effect of the entire scenarios, but I strongly believe that certain treatments handed to certain people; in this context, one's origin and ethnicity – African, plays a more significant role than we care to admit. I know there are similar stories and images we know of, existing in Southeast Asia about child labor, and the clear disregard for children's rights but is it not that the similarities can be summed up as one to demean human beings in order to treat them so?

I try repeatedly to emphasize the point I have always raised, which is: the more pathetic the stories and images are presented, the more connectivity these organizations will get from the "outside world", and yes, it might be so, but my personal direct dialogues randomly with people, convinces me otherwise. However, some of these organizations will simply not agree. Further interesting observation I have made though, is the significant importance it is to their cause, for them to continue this path.

Feeling superior, or being made to feel inferior are not necessarily traits significant with a certain particular group of people, a race, or of a specific ethnicity but I would say, is very human.

We see it in our everyday lives, and live with it without necessarily pointing it out. We even experience it in the animal world through their interactions. In short, it is "normal", and needs no extra vigilance in going about our daily lives and routines. Where I am concerned and seriously affected, is when actions are deliberate and concoctive in order to serve a purpose or reach a goal.

It is obvious that the creation of this world we live in is not based on equality, and should not. It is man's doing, and extra efforts for some to create and maintain superiority over others in their quest to achieve power and dominance.

Slavery is a great example of a man's dominance over others, but how and where is the beginning? In my humble opinion, if and when images and stories are displayed and told over and over again, the belief of the message is founded, creating a life of its own.

As cynical as this might sound, I have often projected a scenario of me going out into the public and engaging people for their honest response to a question as to what first comes to mind when they hear the name "Africa", or when they see images of black kids and adults in a rather familiar environment of filth, degradation, misery, and hopelessness. Without a flinch, I can state categorically that their responses will be that in line with some of what has been mentioned immediately above, if not worse.

I am taking advantage of a very serious and chaotic situation unfolding on the European continent relating to a massive influx of refugees/asylum seekers and migrants, presumably from Syria, Iraq, Afghanistan, North, and Northeast Africa.

It started with massive daily sailing across the Mediterranean in their attempts to reach the borders of Southern Europe, notably Italy and Greece. There are continuous reports and images of desperate refugees/asylum seekers and migrants forcing their ways from Turkey into Greece, as well as some via the Baltic States with the hope of entering into the European Union through Hungary. It looked like the reports and images were not being as sympathetic to the views and feelings of the majority of Europeans, however, predictable, dramatic and disturbing photos and images of a dead little Kurdish boy (apparently from the city of Kobane in Syria) washed ashore on a Turkish beach and had seemingly been ignored by people who came across it, changed people's reactions. In a daring act, somebody boldly picked up this dead boy's body from the shore and this act obviously made headline news on television, news media and the social media in around the world and as expected, changed public opinion in favor of the desperate refugees/asylum seekers and migrants. Germany and Austria, in defiance and ignoring the very same laws that they have significantly contributed in setting up regarding the procedures of immigration and asylum seeking, gave orders for the free thoroughfare of all the masses of women, children, and men, irrespective of their backgrounds.

My need to mention the above serious event here in this piece of writing is to compare a similar and possibly a more cynical situation in direct relationship with the topic of this chapter. It is the story that I have already raised in another part of this book, which I am sure is known to very few people, the story befittingly dubbed: 'The Vulture and the Little Girl'.

I do not remember this image reaching as many people outside of where it had taken place and gathering so much sympathy, plus, yielding the massive positive reactions as the dead Kurdish boy's image and the story has done. Am I tempted to ask how and why it is so? Of course, I am, and my reasons are nothing short of the belief that "Africa and Africans" are unimportant and 'sub-human'. I dare ask whether 'The Vulture and The Little Girl' incident dating back well over 2 decades ago has had any positive impact on the lives of the South-Sudanese, not on the ones who are still displaced due to the unfortunate volatile political upheaval involving the established North, or the refugees who time and again struggle with famine. Well, the answer is 'no'. What can be expected? I am yet to experience a person or people that I randomly converse with on this subject, who know or can recollect such story. My conclusion is that I am not in the least surprised, given the circumstances surrounding the depiction of Africa, south of the Sahara, and "Africans" by the rest of the world community.

In recent weeks, I have keenly observed some news developments in Copenhagen of an organization known in Danish as 'Verdens Bedste Nyheder', or 'World's Best

News' as translated into English. There was a recording of some members of this organization in some sort of 'A happening' at the town hall square, with the goal being: the spread of positive news from different parts of the world, in counter-acting what they refer to as the usual media daily news containing many "sensational and negative" material in light of the on-going influx of asylum-seekers/migrants to Europe. As expected, a media and communications representative of this organization was invited to the morning show off one of the national TV stations to be interviewed. She, of course, for all positive intentions, was quick in narrating, in short, some of what they consider to be positive news. She was forthright in her presentation of the various positive news and developments around the world which her organization considers left out by the international media in giving their usual news. 'The decline in childbirth especially in "Africa', 'the increase in children receiving schooling around the world; 'the positive result in the fight against child labor', 'the decline in malaria cases in sub-Saharan Africa due primarily to the efforts of the United Nations in supplying mosquito nets to families in this area", and more.

I wished I had been part of such an interview as I would have asked some questions. Naturally, the reaction of the TV host was that of elation to hear such 'positive' news considering the grim reality unfolding in Europe.

I, therefore, allowed myself to call this lady up on the telephone to present her with my concerns regarding the apparent positive information they have from places around the world, for the simple fact that I do not believe, based on all the information 'on the ground' in many of the sub-Saharan African communities, that there are any so-called positive news. On the contrary, there is every indication of disillusionment and stagnation, that marks and point to the fact that there is less positive development for the common person in these communities, in light of the natural and human resources known to be available, as well as the potential in these communities.

I cannot help myself but to mention, the similar situations facing the predominantly Syrian, Iraqi and Afghan asylum seekers presumably seeking protection and shelter from the wars, persecution and hunger in their countries, to those widely experienced in some regions on the African continent, without the least of such positive reception being afforded those, involved in the current asylum-seeking saga unfolding in Europe.

In the nation of Mali and parts of North-West Africa, the conflicts from wars (tribal, religious, etc.), plus, lack of proper management of the refugee camps under the control of the United Nations wing responsible, has left many refugees very desperate, and very similar to that which has triggered this mass exodus of people looking for better opportunity in Europe. The livelihood, community lives and the foundation of the Tuareg people of this region have been shattered for years as a result of what has been mentioned above, and the natural havoc from the regular sandstorms which contributes to the devastation of their essential shelter, foods and livestock, leaving them homeless and having to deal with massive famine. This situation is and has been at a status-quo for as long as I can remember and unsurprisingly, is the exact same situation in the Northeastern Kenya, bordering

Somalia and not to forget the plight of South-Sudanese who seem to have this as a permanent status. Whatever the United Nations department that oversees and is responsible for issues of this nature facing the world's unfortunate people is not doing, is really working. I am not shying from stating that the nomad lifestyle of many ethnic people on the African continent cannot always be that borne out of culture and customs but by the unfortunate lack of assistance and help given to other humans elsewhere.

'The world is looking away from the problems facing the majority of people on the African continent (especially those from regions south of the Sahara), similar to problems and issues that have triggered massive support from Europe and the Americas, and other parts of the world', I keep saying to myself. Am I wrong, or is it a hasty conclusion on my part?

Looking at the events unfolding these days regarding especially the social aspects of life across the world, it's evident of the tendency for Western Europe to be a more preferred destination for both refugees and migrants alike, from notably Syria, Afghanistan and Iraq due apparently, to the wars that have been on-going there. There is also an inflow of refugees and migrant from some regions in Asia, Middle East and Africa as well with similar claims as a basis for their need to flee. As erratic and unconventional the various individual European nations' systems of acceptance are, I cannot help but to notice how often it is repeated that those asylum-seekers considered 'economic migrants' must be sorted out and returned to their countries. Strangely enough, this decision affects more than any others, those mainly from diverse African countries – south of the Sahara.

In some of the arguments to support what I refer to as the "sorting out" procedure, there are a group of people more preferred due presumably to them having a better education than others. I remember in the beginning when the recent refugee crisis involving a great number of Syrians and Iraqis fleeing wars and persecution back in their countries, I experienced an unofficial campaign by people sympathetic to their causes, stating how the integration process would not be that challenging due to the 'high educational foundation' many of these Syrians have, from their country. It was often mentioned in the news media of the benefits of welcoming these Syrian refugees into the society as a great number of them were medical Doctors, Engineers, Teachers, Computer Graduates or other academicians. I was not in the least surprised why especially "Africans" were not that welcoming. Your guess, I am sure, is as good as mine in concluding who fall victim to this scenario.

The notion that "Africans" have no education is no surprise. Thanks to the various countless campaign advertisements regularly depicting "Africans" needing the basic fundamentals of schooling, is no news in underlining such notion. Are people outside the various societies on the African continent – south of the Sahara even aware of the fact that there are indeed educational and high educational institutions existing in these African countries, giving both basic and advanced academic education to their people? By the sheer weight of all the bombardment of the negative images presented on "Africa", can one expect any different?

For a number of years, I have concluded that (despite the expected denial from a number of people due to different reasons) being "African" has definitely a demeaning, less-of-a-human, condescending tone and image associated to it. As mentioned in some parts of this book, the only knowledge most people have of "Africans" is what has been presented in the various information mediums, e.g. movies, documentaries, books, magazines, etc. In depicting the numerous news, images, sound and picture recordings, I cannot really blame them for their rather unfortunate opinions of "Africa" and "Africans".

Still on the subject of the on-going massive and excessive migration to Europe, it's just been reported that the European Union leaders are having a summit meeting in Malta with their counterparts from the African continent, on the very important discussion of them persuading (through extensive financial and economic aid) the African leaders in helping to take back their various citizens who are attempting to migrate, along with many others, to their home countries.

I cannot help but wonder as to why, seemingly, all efforts are made by the authorities in the European countries to tackle the sending home of all the Africans as some sort of a priority. I ask myself, if the sending home of the Africans was so important to the leaders of these European countries, that an urgent and immediate action had to be taken whiles the influx of many desperate immigrants, supposedly from areas with conflicts of war, spins out of control for some of the European countries. As pointed out earlier, very similar, if not even worse conditions are being experienced daily on the African continent, just as the given reasons for the welcoming gesture given to the refugees and immigrants by the European countries. It's so obvious that "the Africans" should not be part of the picture in the struggle for acceptance by the desperate refugees and immigrants in Europe, despite the seemingly equal reasons and concerns for their flight for refuge and acceptance in primarily Europe.

In the midst of all the chaos in Europe due to the massive influx of refugees and immigrants, it is no marvel to see the reactions of various governments and government leaders of these European countries directly and indirectly affected.

Amongst many of the observations I have made, is the attention being directed at 'the wrong immigrants', as was the reference made by the Danish Prime Minister in a speech he gave at his party's annual meeting. Other government representatives have made comments directly showing their displeasure of having all the refugees from Africa, who according to them, do not qualify for refugee status but are 'economic migrants' in search of a better life in Europe. In light of such reactions from the European authorities, I dare ask whether they have any concerns for all the other refugees and immigrants who have entered into the European territories and whether they are indeed the genuine refugees they claim to be.

In my interpretation of the unfolding scenarios, being African automatically disqualifies any possibility of acquiring a refugee or immigrant status.

In these times of pressure and confusion due to the on-going tension from the state of alertness around the world due to current heightened terroristic activities in Paris, Copenhagen, Brussels, California, and from the pressing refugee situations in Europe, a lot of insight contribution in the news from people who are close to the sources are very welcoming and sought after. I see various news media on TV, Radio, newspapers and internet utilizing the services, insight and knowledge of these experts.

Original Syrians, Afghans, French, Belgians, Americans, etc. but never, or seldom have I seen a national from these African countries being consulted with, for information sourcing of the issues at stake. Is this act by chance?

Some of the very significant comments I often heard during the initial stages of this current refugee and immigrant issue in Europe which understandably triggered debates across many European communities, were some positive contributions in support of the Syrians, especially. 'They are highly educated,' was one particular comment I heard a lot.

The significance of such comments by moderate supporters of such immigration is that the 'educated' will easily fit into the countries they are migrating to, which in itself is welcoming to the said country and that being 'highly educated' makes it highly probable of easily adjusting to the said country, not forgetting the fact that these European countries are themselves publicly propagating for positive contributions that can add to their goal of building an educated society.

The mention of 'educated people' I would say, should clearly disqualify 'the Africans', should it not? "Africa" & education would not be a situation to consider when referring to the "Africa" the world has come to know, and as sarcastic as I try to be in this instance, I would bet that many of the developed societies outside of the African continent would not even dare dream of "Africa" having 'educated' citizens. How could that be? In light of the image we know of "Africa:"?

I will bet, the knowledge that many societies on the African continent, south of the Sahara, do regularly produce highly educated people in the form of medical Doctors, Engineers, Lawyers, Scientists, Statesmen, etc., from some advanced educational institutions, but sadly never mentioned or written about. It would greatly surprise a great majority of people from the international community!

In Ghana, and I am sure as in many other independent nations on the African continent in post-colonial periods, we were introduced to academic schooling system as practiced by the last colonial government, along the same or similar systems as is back in their home country. The most significant being the language, which is intended to replace the local languages.

It is important to mention that the colonial powers had apparently disregarded the fact that these African countries are by nature, split up along tribal lines and backgrounds. Such drastic action taken lightly by the colonial governments could only be justifiable in the eyes of the international community, by the cruel and twisted presentation of the natives as sub-humans (to be moderate), or even non-humans, who should to be cultivated and made civil.

It was, as it still is, very important to be 'schooled'. To be enrolled into the school system which is primarily still in the language introduced by the colonial governments, such as in English, French, Portuguese, etc., was thought of as both prestigious and an opportunity for the natives. The ability to learn to speak and communicate in the introduced language was and still is considered a great achievement, which carries an extraordinary recognition by the local communities. It must be mentioned that the wide gap created by the division of the ones that have been 'schooled', and the ones who have not, has contributed immensely to the birth of the classes of society, which brings with it the ugly face of inequality. In various communities across the African continent, it is a common sight to see and experience the unfortunate effects this ideology has had.

As mentioned in other parts of this book, the majority of the locals who have not had the 'luck and opportunity' to be 'schooled', are looked down upon and even considered inferior by some of the other 'lucky and fortunate' ones.

I have been brought up in a home which was governed by rules and regulations laid down by my grandmother, who was also the head of the family. My grandmother was 'educated' during the British colonial period in Ghana's history. She went through the strict colonial introduction of education, which included the use of physical force in guiding the schooling; which in many circles worldwide these days is considered an abuse. She was a specimen and a product of the indoctrination that every aspect of life introduced by the colonial government was superior to that of the locals.

She, therefore, held all efforts to learn the ways of colonial masters, in high standards.

I remember how the foundation of my upbringing became a subconscious catalyst for my looking down on others who, in my opinion and supported by my view of the world of classes, were non-inclusive. This, I believe, was by no means a developed habit exclusive to me alone. The feeling of superiority to others in the community was (in looking back) automatic.

I have had a few discussions on the meanings of superiority and inferiority complexes, and I am convinced about the wide perceptions and interpretations amongst many, and as much as I agree with the general understanding of both superiority and inferiority complexes, I am inclined to differ in some of the interpretations.

Contrary to common popular belief and perception of what inferiority complex amongst people of dark color means, I believe, based on collective as well as individual interpretation, that it has more than one meaning. The most common interpretation that I come across daily is that of being accused of presenting or expressing an attitude of liking or in agreement with, and having any form of admiration for the white race. I think it's equally an indication of having a complex of being inferior to others when one takes either defensive or offensive positions just based on the automatic assumption that a random act, or a statement presented by someone of another race is solely racially motivated. In other words, being sensitive to an act or statement due justifiably, to an earlier experience can, in my opinion, is a sign of feeling less about oneself.

This must be substituted for the same feeling and reactions of exactly the opposite description. In my opinion, a common and significant act of inferiority complex is when people who obviously have low self-esteem of themselves and their environments, or a sense of inadequacy, would act in derogatory ways towards others to make themselves feel superior. An example is looking down on others. Repeatedly presenting the very "bad" side of another in making a point, can be another good example.

I have often said that illiteracy is a disease created and passed on to Africans by the colonial powers. Although it is known through history that other parts of the world were colonized, resulting in the introduction of some languages substituting that of the local's and yet there is no other place where illiteracy has been made to transcend even the essence of being human. In my opinion, illiteracy amongst Africans seems to be the link by which lots of judgments, opinions and conclusions are formed about them and seems to have a "double-edge-sword-effect" on the communities as a whole. On one hand we are all aware of the importance of education for the individual and for the community as well, and on the other hand, the wide gap created by the majority of those who for one reason or the other, do not get the same academic education and those who do. There is, of course, the big difference between what I would refer to as an academic education and the general natural education.

I dare claim (though with some amount of reservation) that the remnants of colonial era: portraying and making the "African" think less of themselves as humans by the white man, is quite evident in the way the continent of Africa and Africans – south of the Sahara has been, and is still being treated to the present.

I remember so well during my early boarding school days in post-independent Ghana, most of the depictions of the locals and their interactions, were nothing short of the locals always presented as being subservient to the white colonial 'Masters'. This, I can attest, was the same occurrence in other sub-Saharan African countries. Apart from certain few documented literature showing the struggles, the positive side of the locals and their resistance to the colonial powers and their occupation, everything else was showing the locals in the '2nd class role'. Apparently, all important decisions concerning the handling and development of the communities are taken by the colonial government and their appointees.

This is like 'fast-forward' in my observation of the summary I have of Africa now, and in the past! As far back as I can remember and even to this day, I am yet to document a habit of any of the international news medium involving the locals, when reporting on news relating directly to events which has to do with the said African country. Often when news breaks, the news networks do consult with the locals for 'first-hand' information, and this happens regularly with many parts of the world except with sub-Saharan African countries. I must remember to add, though, that some U.S. news networks, notably CNN, as well as a few other networks, have been doing better in recent times in this area. I have enviously wondered why it is so with Africa, when people supposed to be related to the particular country or region, are consulted with, and allowed to inform and enlighten the world. This is mysteriously not so, in dealing with "Africa" & "Africans".

As I have mentioned elsewhere in this book, it is common to see and witness sports pundits commenting on sporting events (especially football/soccer) involving Africans and African countries south of the Sahara, even though they have little or no knowledge of the said people and countries. Often, these sportsmen and women are strangely referred to with a pronoun, as if they are an unknown species or aliens from another planet. I would think less of such a situation except that these pundits do use derogatory and patronizing comments in commenting on the events, as well as the participants. In my effort to elaborate this point, I cannot let it pass without the mention of the rules used by the football/soccer world governing body; FIFA. Without really knowing the real reason behind the change of rules, FIFA amended some of their rules to allow the continent of Africa the current 5 slots from the previous 2, which had even been only 1 slot prior to that, and in consideration of the great number of countries. Could the reason for the earlier rule be that the African continent did not deserve the representation matching the number of independent nations, or some other reason? Your guess could be as good as mine.

Many expatriates living in many African countries during both, the pre and pro-independent eras had very significant attitudes and 'upper-class' mentalities, similar to those of the colonial Governors. Clear examples can be traced with the large Indian and Middle Eastern settlers who themselves had been by large, subjects of the colonial rule back in their own countries, years before their arrivals in many sub-Saharan Africa for "greener pastures", and their often display of superiority characteristics and upper-class mentality towards the locals.

In consideration of the images and pictures of "Africa" and "Africans" portrayed around the world, it rarely surprises me to hear and see often the comments and attitudes of other communities around the world, of a feeling of being superior human beings compared to "the African" locals. This, in my humble opinion is ridiculous, considering that these communities are in no necessarily & significantly better conditions and environment than "the African".

As debatable as it can be, a great majority of people around the world would (if asked) not hesitate to conclude that "Africans", most probably occupy the last position in a poll on a scale to determine the essence and meaning of being human; with the top being the picturesque image in our brains of everything "the African" is not. This opinion of mine is, of course, with some reservation in relation to people's honesty and sincerity.

I have noticed more and more in recent times when looking through and reading the various articles and news summaries coming out of most African countries, I get confused from some images and attitudes being displayed.

Unless I am hastily making conclusions, it seems to me that many (especially the younger generation) has taken to portraying themselves or rather, seemingly displaying attitudes and characteristic of lifestyles and trends seen in some developed countries like the United

States of America and the United Kingdom, and the Western culture as a whole.

To mention a few, some African countries, notably Nigeria, Ghana, Kenya and others, seem to portray a sense of empowerment by presenting themselves in ways not reflective of their own natural environments, but rather that of the developed societies as mentioned above. It is important to mention that this development seems to be more rampant with the younger generation who for some reason, like to imitate the personalities, characters, cultures, lifestyles and traditions, which apparently boosts their egos, making them feel acceptable and superior in their local environments. It is fair to mention that the introduction of the internet and other internet-based social networks could be an underlining factor as one of the causes of such development. Picking up trends that influences the development and growth of societies is in itself is universal and therefore, is no flaw per say, however, when traditions and norms are discarded by certain people choosing to apply and even try to substitute their own for others, in their conscious efforts to feel good about themselves, as well as to be acceptable in the eyes of others in the society, then I sense a sign of some sort of a complex; a serious human flaw.

The definition of 'education' is one that needs an elaboration in relation to "Africans". In my discussions with people on this subject, I get the feeling that there is a sense of misunderstanding. I believe there should be a clear presentation of what the meaning of education is.

In relating specifically to the challenge faced by sub-Saharan African communities, it is often indicated that illiteracy forms a sound foundation for the lack of development dominant in these said communities and therefore, 'schooling' (academic education) has often been advocated as a solution, and a goal.

As truthful as it might be, I have an issue with the use and meaning of 'schooling' and 'education' as it's presented. I have the personal opinion that the meanings of both school and education can be diverse. Without claiming to have any form of expert knowledge on various forms of schooling methods introduced in many of the African countries, I know that a great majority of the schools apply the introduced colonial languages in tutoring; English, French, Portuguese, etc. and thereby create a tendency for feeling superior over their 'subjects'.

My point in this is that whereas academic achievements and goals can be directly linked to 'schooling', I do differ in the common opinion that a positive life achievement is attributed solely to academic education. In many of the communities across sub-Saharan Africa, there are traces of decent and advanced forms of governance that has been the foundations upon which different cultures and traditions have been built, before and after the arrival of the colonial governments, and very fair to say boldly, that such feats have been without the introduction of the education, as commonly perceived by many. Being educated does not have to be attributed (in this case) to the arrival of the colonial powers to Africa.

It is evident in many of the communities in sub-Saharan Africa of very advanced forms of social, economic, and political structure that forms the foundation of development, and that, it is among the myths that, lack of academic education is one of the major underlining causes of the woes faced by "Africans".

Knowledge is an education! Knowledge is power and by that saying, it must be insulting to humanity, for some to conclude that "Africans" are inferior due in some ways, to their lack of 'knowledge'; not achieved necessarily through academic schooling or education.

In outlining some of the situations which, in my opinion, depict clear examples of complexes of feeling superior to "the African"; high-level meetings usually involving people, organizations, countries, etc., with the intention of providing Aid and assistance to "Africa" tends to be without representation from the affected communities, or from their perspectives. It usually is a gathering of the representations from the developed countries, usually taking decisions and having conclusions, seemingly without consideration and inclusion for, and of, the people whom the said issues are about. This is what I refer to as a classic instance of a 'knowing-what-is-best-for-you' position, which is so evident in so many diverse ways, even to this present time, though appearing in many disguises.

A distinct characteristic of being vestiges of colonial rule, of which I am shamefully a product of, is the ease with which we look down on our own; our people, our efforts, our work and our thinking. It takes no effort, nor does it take a serious evaluation on our part to discard our own in comparison with anything 'non-African'. I remember as a kid growing up in post-colonial and post-independent Ghana and witnessing remnants of colonial thinking being very vivid in our mentalities in executing our daily duties. The habits of accepting, embracing, admiring, being adulatory in our attitudes towards work and products representing and signifying non-Ghanaian, "non-African" and certainly relating to the colonial era, was a very common trait then, and worse, even to this day. Gone are those days when some goods manufactured by local Ghanaians had the inscriptions altered and manipulated to read 'made in England', 'made in Germany', 'made in Japan', etc. to be saleable to the local consumers. This attitude, though is worse in these present times regarding goods and services not only from Western Europe and North America as was the trend then, but from all parts of the world, as long as it's non-local.

Products, goods and services made in "Africa" by "Africans" are usually considered inferior and not – quality. This I would say is a common perception unfortunately by the "Africans" as well, in reflecting on the mindset of people the world over.

An interesting and vivid experience clearly befitting such characters is that of the Carpenter in my neighborhood back in Kumasi, in the Ashanti region of Ghana, where I grew up. He was by all means very good and gifted at his craft (as many locals are, in diverse crafts). He loved his work and the results of his craftsmanship were admired by all who were lucky to be witness to it. The use of his hands on pieces of wood which he admirably transformed into pure work of art was simply sublime. During school breaks when I came home from boarding school, I was honored to be part of a group of boys he gathered for an important chore; getting us to inscribe on rulers he had made of wood. Though

170

there was always an air of confidence in producing these rulers, it was clear to us that he had a hard time selling them. This, we all believe, was due greatly to the rulers being locally produced, thus, all the efforts in getting us to hand write: a 'Made in England' inscription on them after he was through with the finishing procedures. He did succeed in selling lots of the rulers he had produced in the local markets.

Without needing to refer to the various technicalities within international trade, which in itself can present an intricate mechanism, the world could not have been turning a blind eye to the numerous occasions, where prices and demand of highly demandable consumer products internationally, from African countries, which often is the foundation of the economies of many of these countries, are manipulated and sabotaged by consumer nations abroad, in efforts to influence the prices and terms to their benefits, despite the adverse and devastating effects it has on the producing countries on the African continent. Coffee, Cocoa, etc., to mention a few, are clear examples, and it is no secret who controls the movements of the foreign currencies which give support to every strong economy.

I read a presentation brochure from an established chain jewelry dealer in London a while back in which they had, for advertisement purpose I guess, introduced a selective layout on their diamond jewelry collection. In their effort to achieve their goals, they had undertaken to present a story of how the diamonds got to the stage as displayed in the brochure and I must point out the uneasy feeling I had at the time. In graphics, animation, and in color, they had tried to detail the route from the rough diamond mined in South Africa, through the transportation to a specific country in Europe where the pre-jewel processing stage had taken place.

In all of this narration, the people who were apparently physically involved in this whole process were shown in detail, except the mention and depiction of the very important role played by the local South African miners. As many will agree with me, being physically in the mines and digging out the rough stones is, without a doubt, an integral and very important part that completes the cycle. It is important to mention that this is but one of many examples showing the intent to make the being and existence of "the African", and the relevant important contribution to positive developments, irrelevant.

One very notable observation I have a good memory of, is the relations between the developed countries, and people from the continent of Africa. Western Europe and North America are without a doubt the most preferred destinations for most people from the African continent with the intent to either travel to study, or just immigrate. Whether this tendency has any direct or indirect bearing on the colonial past is hard to tell, but I can certainly conclude that the influence in making, especially the people from sub-Saharan Africa feel 'special' about themselves in this regard, is not difficult to sense. It is important not to generalize, but I would say that due probably to the effects colonialism has had on the various societies in sub-Saharan Africa, it (as mentioned in other places in this book) is no surprise, of the overly and sometimes exaggerated admiration they (people from sub-Saharan Africa) have for Westerners.

Without it being that of a surprise to me, that majority of the societies which have been directly affected by colonialism would exhibit some degree of behavioral complex towards the societies that colonized them, it does still surprises me to experience a very significant trait visible amongst those, especially from sub-Saharan Africa, in their adopted countries – due to immigration, studying, or even for other non-permanent errands, themselves displaying attitudes of superiority towards their fellow countrymen back in their home countries. Without any intent to offend anyone, we all in one way or the other have (some in more conscious ways than others) at some time, felt and shown the feeling of 'being special', and 'privileged' because we live, study, or have traveled to the U.K., the U.S.A., to Germany, etc.

As much as it might be difficult for some of us to admit, I have no doubt that this is a very common and significant character.

It is worth mentioning that characters, as described immediately above, are an ego booster for those of us domiciled in the western societies (though many would not admit), and are made worse by the thinking and reception by those living back in our home countries. I am not shy to mention how some of us behave in ways of being superior to those back in our home countries, sometimes worse than the "non-Africans" did and still do, just because of our associations with the societies abroad. This is especially so in the regions south of the Sahara, relating especially with the western societies. I am inclined to summarize on how such character, borders that of having a bloated self-belief of being superior,

173

when one goes around with the twisted feeling and attitude of being a better human being than the next.

A vivid memory I still have of my youth was the fascination of seeing movies and the various effects it had on me. Those were the era of the 'black and white' movies. The days of the Charlie Chaplin, Buster Keaton, Tarzan, and the others, however, a particular experience still lingers on in my head. The screen adaptation of the character: 'Tarzan'.

Tarzan was a fictitious character created by an American. He, Tarzan, was white and a descendant of the aristocracy, who was mysteriously marooned in "Africa" as an infant and had to be raised by Apes to survive and save the world. He obviously had to survive by adapting to the life of the Apes. He learned to do everything like the Apes did, living in the jungles of Africa. The Tarzan character is simply to put it, a hero and a super-human with the abilities to save the world. I remember already then at a young age, the strange feeling of having a white man in that role.

'I would love so much to be in that hero position,' I often thought and said to myself but I was quick in reminding myself of whom I was; an "African"; a black boy. Already then, the conclusion I often came to was that one must have to be 'white' in order to attain any position of importance in a movie, as I struggled with the understanding of why a white man is playing the role of 'the king in the jungles of Africa'.

Among others, these personal questions I harbored in my mind concerning the role of the white person in my community, in storybooks, and ultimately in movies, were no more confusing, thinking of how a number of teachers, both in my own boarding school as well as other schools, were white people.

'Could a black man from an African country not play the role of Tarzan instead?' I often wondered.

'If only I was older, I would definitely be a better Tarzan,' I did say to myself.

So many years have gone by when I used to view the role of Tarzan played by a white man with envy and felt even worse realizing that it could never be.

Fast forward to the present time, and we witness the roles of Tarzan many times fold. Unless one is living under a rock somewhere, there is no situation befalling sub-Saharan Africa and its people needing help that do not require either by choice or otherwise, the direct involvement of Europeans, Americans, Japanese, Chinese (of late), and a whole lot of people countries outside of the African continent. To put it mildly, actions around the world have created a deep notion that everyone else outside of the African continent but the sub-Saharan Africans themselves, are the saviors.

Interestingly, both the people from sub-Saharan Africa and those from outside the African continent, especially from the so-called 'developed world', believe this to be so.

It is saddening to observe from afar, via global news, and also feel through direct associations with people from the sub-Sahara region of the African continent, the mental effect of such actions; making people feel powerless over their own lives and making others the 'Lords of their destinies', while whites on the other hand - 'the Lords', utilizes this power to the fullest and beyond, and plus, the feeling of having total control of the lives of others.

I have stated many times of how it usually is easier to recognize clear exhibitions of superiority towards dark-skin people from sub-Sahara Africa in the way comments are made about them in certain sports competitions.

Football/soccer is one sporting event that stands out in my mind in relation to the way people act superior when dealing with dark-skin people of sub-Saharan Africa. Being a sports enthusiast and a football/soccer fanatic, I remember years back when it was very normal not to witness football/soccer games outside the continent of Africa involving dark-skin people from sub-Saharan Africa. It was, therefore, no surprise that the interest in this sport involving people from sub-Saharan Africans was non-existent in places outside of the African continent.

Not only was it of no interest to the outside world, it was even not permitted. This, I must remember to point out, was not relating only to dark-skin people from sub-Saharan Africa but to dark-skin people in general.

Though no official reason has been given over time as to why it was so, it is obvious to many who care to know the real truth behind such actions. Black people, to some (who know no better) no matter where they originate, are often ignorantly considered "Africans" and therefore, inferior human beings incapable of participating in the sports that the Europeans were doing. This must be why the sport of football/soccer had no dark-skin people from sub-Saharan Africa participating for decades until recently, now be more acceptable.

Not forgetting the historical background of the continent of Africa in colonial times and the influence of expatriates, the sport of football/soccer which is no exception, has developed over time and thereby attracting interest from outside the African continent as well. What I have noticed over a long time is the so-called experts and pundits always giving the credit of success to the various teams or to the expatriate Coaches, in situations where the various countries engage expatriate Coaches. I am yet to hear any of the commentators, the so-called experts and pundits giving credit to the teams from sub-Saharan Africa for their team efforts without making mention of how the European Coaches' infusion of discipline and tactical discipline has contributed immensely to the successes of the various sub-Saharan African teams. As it's always been, the "African" is incapable of positive achievements and successes without the European's contribution.

In the big tournaments like the FIFA World football/Soccer championships where the best countries who have qualified meet and compete for the ultimate championship price, representations from countries from the African continent was minimal and almost non-existent until a few years back.

Without any significant interest and knowledge of football/soccer played in the African countries, it surprises me each time at such tournaments when the selected experts, pundits, and commentators are usually Europeans, Americans, Japanese, Germans, and from many of countries outside the African continent, and in more ways than one, their condescending comments about the players and teams from especially sub-Saharan Africa.

I often wonder how and when these so-called experts, pundits, and commentators who have not been interested in football/soccer played on the African continent, all of a sudden got the interest and knowledge that had put them in positions where they could guide many football/soccer lovers around the world on the sport as it is on the continent of Africa. I wonder whether these TV and radio networks who hire these so-called experts, pundits and commentators from outside the African continent have no regard for such positions being occupied by someone with first-hand knowledge; someone from either the continent or the said country involved in the game.

Chapter 12
Human Dignity

I have just seen a new TV advert from another of these very established international organizations, presenting someone (probably a known personality in Denmark) presumably traveling through an "African" community – typically with mud and hay huts and semi-clothed kids running around in the background. As a matter of fact, there is also a typical pose of some kids gathered together and seemingly demonstrating the intended message as probably instructed to.

I wish someone will join me in demanding from these supposedly well-intended people and organizations why the need to continuously present Africa this way. In my opinion, the efforts of the people and organizations are bordering and even sometimes, crossing the line into what I have long considered a deliberate and calculated effort to attract and seek pity from potential donors; resulting in their disregard for the basic human dignity of these same "Africans" they claim to be helping.

There was a story years back, during one of the famine situation in the country Sudan, I will guess was in the mid-1990s to1994 to be precise, of a photograph taken by a South African Photojournalist by the name of Kevin Carter, who happened to be at the scene of one of the most memorable events during the very harsh famines that hit the Northeastern region of Africa, as was depicted in news bulletins across the world.

The photograph depicted a very powerful image of the result of such natural disasters that occur periodically around the world and it's very devastating consequences. My understanding is that the goal of the Journalist was his attempt to send an 'alarm' to the rest of the world who had, as usual, turned a 'blind eye' to this disaster occurring in "Africa", for an urgent action in helping to avoid further unnecessary deaths among the affected. I remember debating on some occasions with other interested people on whether the seemingly frantic effort on his part, which in a way I do understand, was ethical.

A very, very weak and frail Sudanese child, a girl presumably, who seemingly did not have the strength to continue with the other victims of this devastating famine, to probably one of the many temporal centers set up by the United Nations and other help organizations to feed the hungry and the affected, laid down by the wayside. She was seemingly dehydrated, weak and frail, and nothing left of this 'poor' child but skin and bones. There seemed to be other activities nearby, notably from a 'bird of prey' – a vulture! From what we know, vultures are some of nature's most notorious scavengers well known to prey on the flesh and carcasses, stripping them completely off. Some other species are even known to devour both flesh as well as bones.

A Vulture had, of course, made its intentions known and was stalking this poor child. It was gradually approaching in their usual short fly-jump motion and fast. Instinctively, I would assume that most of us would go into a protective mode to try to ward off this helpless child from the on-coming vulture and most would probably try to scare it away. Contrary to what I think the majority of us would do, this Photojournalist allowed this Vulture to play out its stalking role whiles the poor, helpless, weak and dehydrated Sudanese child kept lying there in a fetal position.

In pondering over such a scenario being played out and the uncomfortable debate I am having with myself regarding the fine line between cynicism and realism, could the actions of this Photojournalist be that of someone on a mission? The mission to help create a scenario substantive enough for a perfect story; that of an unusually disturbing image of a helpless human being subjected to a very chilling situation which we can only imagine in our worlds, most probably supported by fictitious images from books and films – 'about to be attacked and devoured by an African Vulture – a befitting title I can imagine, for a 'good story' in the news or tabloids.

The Photojournalist gets his 'shot' and thankfully, it goes around in the international media, resulting in a positive shake-up and a wake-up call for the rest of the world, especially in the 'developed countries'. The story goes; no one ever got to know what became of that child, whom I believe, did not have the faintest idea of the strange event that had taken place around her, a short while back. Of course, this very powerful image depicted in a photograph ended in the newspapers of some of the very dominating international media networks, which resulted in eventually help getting to those who needed it.

I allowed myself to believe that this photograph of the Sudanese girl was necessary to send a powerful appeal to the rest of the world who had before then, not really shown any interest whatsoever, however, would you react on your instincts and run to the aid of the girl and chase the vulture away, or you would have done the same as the Photojournalist – Kevin Carter, if you were in his position. As a matter of interest, Mr. Kevin Carter was awarded the prestigious Pulitzer Prize for that piece of work. He sadly passed away (reportedly from committing suicide) some few months after this episode.

I see a serious dilemma in this from my point of view, and I wonder whether others see it my way.

In Denmark, as in a great number of the so-called 'developed countries', it is a common sight to see through various campaign ads via all forms of media, on the need for monetary contributions to aid the 'poor & suffering Africans'. The pictures and images of "African" kids and adults in all forms, are constantly presented almost on daily basis by the countless aid organizations and their partners.

I have lost count of how many times I have had to call to some of these aid organizations in relation to one form or the other of their numerous campaign advertisements, only to be met with their usual defensive and patronizing positions. Even in their attempts to be understanding to the concerns I raise, I am yet to see any active attempt to be sympathetic to the inhuman image and pictures presented. On the contrary, the intensity of the various adverts from some of the big and major aid organizations in pushing their message through to the public, cuts across as being a competition amongst themselves for presenting the most heartbreaking, pathetic, degrading and unworthy-of-a-human type of images, pictures and messages.

'The meaner and degrading the messages are, the better,' is how I would classify them.

On my way out into town the other evening, I saw one of the usual ad-posters from one of the major 'players' – 'Boernefonden' (Children Fund) on their usual aggressive campaign appeals to the general public to help "Africa/the Africans". The message from this particular poster read: 'give hope to a young person in Africa', and showing the face of a black person with a look depicting misery and despair. A sub-message on the same poster is appealing as well to the public to 'support the youth's way out of poverty in Africa'. As I often do, my reaction was to get in touch with this organization and make them aware again, on the concern some of us have in relation to the negative image of the African continent and its consequences, which I did.

A female representative – a Marketing Consultant that I ended up talking to on the telephone, along with disagreeing as usual to my concerns, and in an irritated tone, uttered the following: 'I come in every day, and work hard to help these poor people,' which sounded arrogant in my opinion.

I had requested a personal meeting with them to make them aware of the consequences of some of their ad campaigns to attract monetary donations from the Danish public, which I had done several times before; however, it was not going to happen. In responding to an email message she had decided to send to me instead, in which she had recommended me to visit their website and see their program (not mentioning even a single one of the concerns I had raised)... The very same programs, some of which had concerned me. I indicated to her that her/their reaction and response could only be that of, either not wanting to be bothered or just not caring.

I may be wrong, but from the angle I am looking in on the various campaigns for monetary support from the general public, by almost all the numerous aid organizations (some more than others), the more sorts ofmisery, poverty and hopelessness that can be displayed, the more sympathy they hope to win.

As much as some of these aid organizations I have contacted, have of course, denied, and will most likely be the same with all the others, it is like them running "a rat race" (in my view) in appearing with images, pictures, inscriptions, etc., that can have the most effect and have the strongest impact. I have, on some occasions, even argued about how cynical some of them are willing to be with their messages in order to achieve their goals – obviously bringing in as much donation as possible.

There are several incidents that have taken place over many years and still taking place in these present times which makes me wonder as to whether "the African" is seen and treated with the same dignity as other people.

One of the most recent significant developments known to the international communities over many years is the illegal transportation and dumping of toxic waste from, and by, the developed countries into some African countries - notably some West African countries, and in Somalia. These practices we know can be both by consent of some of the corrupt officials of the said African countries, and also by the sheer lack of recognition on the part of the developed countries, of the human dignity for the citizens of the African nations – south of the Sahara.

As indicated sporadically in other parts of this book, the words "Africa" or "African" used commonly in referring to dark-skin people originating from the sub-Saharan region of the African continent – which I like to refer to as a term, can be directly linked to the sub-human nature often seen as. In these days of massive refugee and immigrants knocking on the doors of Western Europe and the ensuing chaos it has brought to bear on the European communities, I cannot bear the pain I have in my heart when I see the pressure it has come to bear on the United Nations and the work they do relating to refugees around the world. My on-going feelings do not overlook the fact that the immediate attention by the international community, through the calculated efforts of the United Nations, to provide aid and assistance to the Syrian refugees, directly affects the masses of refugees in similar or worse conditions in the refugee camps in East Africa - Northern Kenya to be more precise. Not to trivialize the plight of the people fleeing Syria, I am obliged to ask why similar attention and assistance is not given by the international community to the refugees in camps in East Africa.

My own curious observation is that the international community might probably not even be aware, but then, why does the United Nations not make similar efforts through their campaigns requesting urgent and immediate action on the part of these refugees in East Africa and elsewhere on the African continent?

I often ask myself why "Africa" and "Africans" are synonymous with negativity. In the everyday thinking, my immediate statement above must be seen as subjective, however, I am allowing myself to view this with a huge dose of realism….because it is real!

In continuing with the subject of immediate International assistance to the known disasters – droughts, famine, wars, displacement, diseases, etc., affecting "Africa/Africans", it is an understatement to say that there is a definite discrimination in the whole approach and set up. It is no secret how often the International community, spearheaded by the United Nations, has been slow in reacting to disaster situations affecting Africa/Africans. Often, it is normal and acceptable to see affected African victims of such man-made and natural disasters in Africa presented in the most inhumane, demeaning, destitute and miserable way.

I dare say that there is little human dignity applied to the unfortunate "African" victims of such disasters on the continent of Africa – south of the Sahara.

This aforementioned behavior of the International community is worrying when it happens over and over again. Disaster situations on the African continent south of the Sahara needing immediate attention and action from the international community usually trigger a non-reaction, or very slow responses, often leading to situations being uncontrollable and often too late for many victims. It usually warrants the un-dignifying pictures and images as mentioned above. It does not seem to be the case with others around the world in similar disaster situations, or is it because the international community sees the "Africa/African" differently?

Many scenes depicting very desperate people in desolate areas in some of the affected areas on the African continent, south of the Sahara are extremely pathetic. There is a question that crosses my mind each time I see any form of an attempt at enforcing, either consciously or sub-consciously, this much founded negative image of Africa and the various citizens of the various African countries, which is: 'how long will this go on?'

I think of the generations that will have to face this battle, in my opinion, being waged on all fronts.

History tells us of how the African continent in post-colonial times was divided up by the colonial powers into communities serving the personal ambitions of these colonial powers, and without having to bring back painful memories, which I strongly believe has been the strongest part of the foundation for which even to this day, influences the daily lives of many of the societies which were colonized. This, therefore, must be the reason why in the least (in my opinion) we do not see the positive results from the colonized era, like socio – developments, advanced educational institutions, good tarred roads, modern buildings, etc. This leads me to ask whether someone, somewhere is better served in presenting these usual pitiful images.

What is the purpose?

What I believe is not being addressed, are the consequences of such actions. There are those who claim the opposite of my conclusion; of course, the humanitarian and aid organizations. Their claim, which is contrary to my conclusion, is that they (through their various ad campaigns) always make sure to show respect to the "Africans" they portray, as well as showing the positive side "Africa", and the "Africans" appearing in their campaigns. This, I humbly disagree, and will dare say that this assertion can be patronizing and insulting to the integrity of many people from the African continent south of the Sahara, when they are being looked down on daily, and deprived of many opportunities given to others, and considered primitive and uncultured, to say the least.

Some of the ways by which "Africans" are daily discriminated upon is in the field of sports, through various comments made about them and in the way they are treated. Numerous documentation exists of people originating from the continent of Africa – south of the Sahara, having been openly treated in negative ways, discriminated on, and made to feel inferior and sub-human. There are many examples of elite sportsmen and women originating from the continent of Africa – south of the Sahara, who are paid less for the same, if not more, of the work they put out.

My research has led me to conclude that many of these innocent hard working people from that part of the world, do accept such treatments due partly to the unwanted hardships back in their countries, and sometimes, as pathetic as it might sound, believe that the said unfair and demeaning treatment is justifiable.

My conclusion relating to this immediate point is that; of constantly being told of how low of a person and inferior you are, being shown images and pictures of yourself and community without dignity, and being bombarded with constant news of negativity about your community and yourself, could definitely be a catalyst to believe it to be true.

The seemingly double standards directly relating to reactions and treatments given to "Africa" and "Africans" in times of need, and call the for assistance during disaster periods, can, in my opinion, be attributed to 2 very significant factors; the conscious and the subconscious. As stated in some sections above, there is a majority of the international community (including, unfortunately, many "Africans") who simply do not know otherwise, on one side, and those who have the knowledge, but manipulates for their personal gains. Ignorance is what I often hear as a primal reason for certain behaviors towards "Africa" and "Africans".

'All we know is what the media portrays,' is the answer I often get when I bring people's attention to some of what I have mentioned in different parts of this book. This goes without saying that the aid organizations have a significant role in such perception by a great number of people in the world and the ensuing results.

In reflecting over some of the many unfortunate incidents that underline this topic, one particular incident comes to mind that has stayed with me even to this day.

Months prior to the year 1998, there had been sporadic reports coming out of East Africa of an impending famine which could have devastating consequences for the inhabitants. These reports were coming from some private, as well as known aid organizations and appearing sparsely in the international media. Apparently, the situation got worsened by the lack of support from the international community to react to the calls coming from East Africa, until the internationally-renowned news network – CNN started reporting in the spring of 1998, often with live reporting, that the world's attention came to bear. This, of course, had been made possible by the intensive presentation of some of the ugly, pathetic and inhumane images and pictures that often characterizes the suffering of the "Africans" in Africa on our televisions, newspapers, and other media forms. One would think that similar devastating incidents of such magnitude and caliber, and even worse, having occurred to citizens on the same continent years prior would have been a learning tool for a change in the attitudes of the international community but no! The response from the international community was slow and non-caring. Unfortunately, many deaths and devastation were witnessed and recorded.

The lack of human dignity for "the African" and "Africans" in general, by especially the Western Media, and to some extent the international media as a whole, is appalling and abominable. In reviewing the seemingly stagnant position taken by the Western media in their portrayal of "Africans", it does often make me wonder what really the "payoff" for them is, in holding such a position which seems to get worse by the years.

Since the start of what I refer to as the wars of the modern era – the wars in Balkan, the Gulf wars in the Middle East, the fight against terrorism or the so-called 'Arab Spring' predominantly in North Africa, there have been military forces from the West, the so-called 'Western Coalition, directly engaged in some form of combat, and other war activities. The inevitable consequences of such engagements being the unfortunate loss of human lives, are all so demonstrated in diverse ways, some of which are the often display of mutilated bodies of fallen soldiers. It is important to mention that such actions, as described here, are usually deliberate and provocative acts against the 'West', who are often targeted for propaganda purposes by the opposing sides; the presentation of dead soldiers in public (some completely or partially naked), the macabre state of dead bodies and bizarre treatment of dead bodies, or the presentation of captured or wounded soldiers seemingly confessing or pleading, all in the efforts to humiliate the 'West'.

In almost all these bizarre and strange images reaching the international community, the faces and bodies of the victims are either completely or partially covered (where necessary), and sometimes, not shown at all. Such efforts and acts to stop the exposure of such images and pictures to the public, are supposedly done in upholding the dignity of these victims.

I have often heard the news presenter mention their decision to either fully or partially cover the victim (in such situations), being the conclusion of serious considerations of dignity and respect to the victim and relatives. In agreeing with such honorable and humane decision, I wonder why the media does not resort to same or similar consideration for the countless victims and relatives of "Africans" in 'compromising' and similar situations, that they more than often are so eager to show the world.

Some months down the line, whilst the struggle was going on to secure help and assistance for the masses of people in parts of Ethiopia and parts of Sudan affected by this disaster, another interesting development was taking place in a remote area in North-America. In the icy waters of Alaska, a trio of whales had been stranded under the vast layer of ice and could not break free, and swim away into their usual environment. The unfortunate ordeal which was noticed by a local who then reported further to the local news representative, and went on to make serious international news which even got the then President of the USA personally involved. The news was given a top priority by the US president, which then got an expensive rescue team and operation mobilized. Within a relatively short time, all available top class and expensive rescue apparatus were put into motion, and this unfortunate tragedy was avoided. The whales were rescued and the story had a happy ending. I remember so well when a Middle-East businessman amazingly responded quickly to calls for monetary donations in efforts to free the whales, and made a cash donation in the form of some millions of US Dollars. As a summary reflecting this ordeal, one of the significant players in the rescue team made the following comment in response to why it was such a 'big deal' with the news, and the efforts to rescue these whales: 'People are like that. It may be an instinct; it is what makes us human. And if there was anything to lament in the colossal effort to save the whales, it was not that we care too much for another species but that too often we care too little for our own.'

This incident had an immediate significant impact on me and affected me so much that I started an organization – 'Continental Africa Image International', to combat what I perceived as a negative and damaging image of the continent of Africa – south of the Sahara, and wrote to some international organizations and diplomatic missions based in Denmark for support. Following is a copy of the letter I sent out:

CONTINENTAL AFRICAN IMAGE - INTERNATIONAL

(A non-Political, non-Profitable Humanitarian Organisation)

H. E. AMBASSADOR
CHARGÉ D'AFFAIRES
HEAD OF MISSION
HEAD OF GOVERNMENT

Nov. 15, 1988

(Temporal Address)
Rantzausgade 21 B., 4 th
DK-2200 Copenhagen N
Denmark
Giro 5 13 90 23

Your Excellency,

The formation and Inauguration of an International Humanitarian Organisation (as a platform), for the protection and uplift of the Image of the African Continent, in relation to the International Community and action against the negative campaign by the International Community to degrade and suppress the dignity of the African.

The Image of the African, Internationally

You will by all means agree beyond all reasonable doubts, that for a long time, being an African is to being in but the most awesome situation in respect to the International Community and especially the so-called 'developed' countries in terms of one's existence as a full HUMAN BEING. In many instances, Africans have been and are still being compared to Apes and in some cases, even lower.

The Negative Campaign by the International Media

One hardly finds any International Newspaper, TV./Radio broadcasts or Magazines that brings out the positive side of Africa. Infact, there is an International Rock-band that has made a song depicting the 'atrocity' being done to the African Continent and Africans with the ff. lyrics: «I'm hearing only bad news/bad news on Radio Africa». Africa, to most part of the International Community is nothing short of place in the wilderness with only problems such as deseases, hunger, poverty, dependency on Aid, wars, suffering, starvation, Chaos, etc., and not in any way contributing to the positive development of this Universe.

The Exploitation of the Natural Disaster Situations in Africa

The call for humanitarian help by various International Bodies and individuals is very much appreciated by Africans and Africa as a whole in times of Natural Disasters, etc. Many a time, the situation has been blown out of proportion by the Media and thereby exploited by the same who activate help, leaving Africa and her suffering citizens in the long run, without much hope whiles they enrich themselves and acclaim fame on the account of the suffering African disaster victims. These hypocritic acts, always does well to erase or cover the positive contributions that the Africans and Africa give to themselves.

The Suppression of the Dignity of the African, Internationally

In many instances, Africans are not considered for many good positions Internationally and abroad even though they are as qualified as others are. In other instances, Africans are being treated inhumanly and made mockery of. The dignity of the African has been and is still being suppressed, and in most cases, are looked on as being incapable of doing anything positive.

The use of Africans both locally and abroad, as Scape-goats for Scientific Experimental failures and Accidents.

It is no secret that a lot of evidence have been found over the years where a lot of scientific experiment

194

have been performed on Africans at home without their full acknowledgment and consciousness. When certain scientific experiments fail in the 'developed' countries thereby bringing about some dangerous effects such as deseases, etc., Africa has on most occasions been picked out as being the source of such dangerous effects. Take the case of some African countries being used as a dumping place for extremely dangerous toxic waste belonging to some developed countries, and there is a strong belief among many Africans that this practice is of old unknowingly to most of us.

The lack of Respect for Africa and Africans despite positive positions and Achievments

In the fields of Sports, Science, Education, Development, Religion, International Services, Struggle for World Peace in which the Africans almost always excelling, it does not take long before such positive achievments are completely forgotten by the International Media. An African, despite what position he/she occupies, is almost always a mockery to the International Community, and more so annoying, to the Black ethnic minorities of other developed countries and elsewhere who by some strange reasons have 'lost their heads and respect' for Africa and Africans, forgetting that their roots lay in the very same place of which they make mockery of

The Mockery of Africans through the Film Media.

There is a side of Africa and Africans that is mostly seen through movies, documentaries, feature films, etc. (that is if it is lucky to have a scene appearance), and that side is that of laughter for those who find it amusing. Even when cartoon films are made for children, the scenes that have something to do with Africa and Africans are that of mockery of the land, its people, their culture, their tradition and various languages of the various sectors of the continent

The variety of Lies told to Discredit the positive existence of the African/Africa by the International Media.

No one but the African should know what Africa really is and what the various lands and its people offer, and can offer. The various traditions and cultures of Africans have been misunderstood and misinterpreted to the International Community as an act of being primitive, uncouth, and savagery. Africans are sometimes in some circles, thought of as being cannibals, savages, etc. Various African traditional shows have been misinterpreted to the International Community as being that of a savagery act or like-wise and yet, the hospitality of Africans is known to be the best in the world. Africans in many instances are being compared to and with animals and Africa, as a Jungle. This has brought about the bad treatment by most of the International Community of Africans, who are considered lower than house pets both in Africa and abroad due to what they hear and get to know of Africa and Africans.

Goals and Objectives of this Organisation.

1. To stand up against the negative campaigns towards Africa/Africans.
2. Campaign for the Promotion of the Image and Dignity of Africa and Africans
3. Promote the positive existence of Africa to the International Community.
4. Help make the Dignity of the African Praiseful/Worthy in the eyes of the International Community
5. To relay to the International Press through probable Legal and other actions, to stop their negative campaign against Africa and Africans
6. To relay to the International Bodies/Individuals through probableLegal and other actions, to stop their negative campaign against Africa and Africans
7. To be of help to Africans who get faced with such kind of atrocities abroad.
8. To help create positive attitude from the International Community and fairness towards Africans abroad and at home, and Africa.
9. To contribute in securing beneficial projects for Africa.
10. To protect and help Africans abroad in respect to their jobs and positions.

Financial Support for the Existence and survival of this Organisation

Due to the peacefull reputation of Scandinavia, their support and contribution towards humanitarian and Universal Peace Movement, we chose Copenhagen - Denmark as the adequate place for the HQ of this Organisation.
There is no doubt however, of the high costs of living in Denmark and all the Scandinavian countries as a whole. In order to operate as a fully recognized Organisation, we need a fully furnished Office with a permanent address and with Office facilities such as telex machine, telephones, typewriting machines, etc., and also some few personnel to work in this establishment. One of the ways of strengthening this Organisation,

and consequently took an action. We were hoping that the result of their action would be seen in the same leading newspaper but due to Diplomacy, we never saw any thing written in any of the newspapers even to this day.

The time has come that such a move be made as it has been a fantasy of many Africans both at home and abroad. Its your task too, and more so to make this dream a reality. Africa and Africans have been far too long on the recieving end, and this must change. Help us to help ourselves Internationally.

The other side of Africa MUST be presented to the International Community and without your contribution, it will remain a fantasy. Many a time, one realises that it feels like being any other race but African is allright. This is a bad feeling and must be erased from within both Africans and the International Community. To be African in many 'circles', is to be dirty, primitive and the lowest of all races on earth. This reputation must not be allowed to remain and it must be counter-acted and changed. The time has come that Africa's Image is raised, Africa's torch is lit, Africa shines in all corners of the earth, the dignity of the African is raised high and brought out of darkness. Your contribution is inevitable.

If you do not act urgently and contribute, this Organisation will never be inaugurated and this letter will be the furthest this idealism will go. We are waiting and counting on your urgent contribution to make this idealism live.

Help us to push the International Media/Bodies/Individuals to do their best in transcending, uplifting, and upgrading the same image and dignity of Africa and Africans that they have done their best in destroying over the years.

Please Your Excellency, do not put this letter away for another time and a later action on it, for if you do, you will be contributing rather in killing this idealism. A lot of effort, time and money has been spent to start this movement. Our next move, which is the urgent Inauguration (which needs funds) of this Organisation depends upon your positive response and action.

If the inauguration, existence and survivial of this Organisation does not become a reality, then at least you know that some of us tried, but that this part that you are to play, will forever remain known, either for the positive or negative.

NB: Something Worth Thinking About:

International Media News, 20/10/88. 3 young grey whales have been trapped in the icy sea of Alaska - U.S.A. Frantic efforts are being made to help them (NB: they are not a dying-out species). Within 24 hrs. there are many contributions physically and financially coming to the aid of the whales. A single donation from source, is about US$ 3.5 million, and the President of the U.S.A. calls to congratulate the contributors. Try to make a connection with that of the whole attitude towards the "drought striken" Ethiopians, by the International Community.

Respectfully,

Cc: All African Diplomatic Missions in Scandinavia - Europe.
     Heads of Governments in all African Countries.
     O.A.U. HQ.

NB: Innauguration Invitations to be sent to:
     All African Diplomatic Missions in Scandinavia - Europe.
     Heads of Governments in all African Countries.
     O.A.U. HQ.
     Governments of all Scandinavian Countries.
     The International Media: TV/RADIO - B.B.C., V.O.A., V.O.G., Moscow.
                               Newspaper - N.Y. Times, Herald Tribune, Etc.
                               Newsmagazine - Time, Newsweek, W. Africa/Africa.

     ENCLD: Giro card.

Chapter 13
The Challenges and the Dilemma

It is no hidden fact that a distinguishing characteristic of all humans on this earth, is having the same aspirations to life; to be healthy, prosperous, long-life, successful, providing and catering for one's kids and families, etc., no matter where we live, or where we are from.

In reflecting on the situation involving "Africa" and "Africans", and the reality of seeing so much suffering, misery, and all the negative nouns that come to mind, it seems impossible for any solution. In speaking with many across different walks of life, it seems like everyone has some sort of a proposition to a lasting solution, however, it always has an inconclusive ending. Where is the answer to all the above-described states that we witness daily, of a particular people in a particular place, who seem to know no joy?

I often ask myself: how it is at all conceivable that a continent blessed with every natural product meaningful to mankind, and proven beyond all reasonable doubts to be the foundations for which all prosperous communities around the globe are built, should have such fate. Why should the communities in "Africa" suffer? I dare state boldly and without equivocation that no amount of unfair treatment relating to "Africa and Africans" is justifiable.

History depicts the various forms of struggles that "Africans" have faced and are still facing. Whiles direct reference to some of the stories (told and untold) relating to the existence and co-existence of "Africans" might not be warranted, it is (in my opinion) worth stating that no other communities have been treated so woefully and gone through so much injustice.

So many efforts have been made by many organizations and activists working in the interest of women, animals, and minorities, and advocating various implementations of various rules and laws to protect and safeguard them, however, I do not see similar propositions or suggestions in making the situation of the "African" better. The seemingly unilateral marginalization of the position of "Africa and Africans" is real, alive and ever so vivid.

In my continuous interest to promote my agenda, I have taken to touch on issues which I hope will contribute to the efforts to locate, address, and act in ways that will affect some changes for the betterment of the innocent, defenseless people from communities in sub-Saharan Africa.

The obvious challenges confronting the sub-Sahara African communities, are enormous and can be traced back to centuries of diverse causes; however, no concrete benefits to the communities have been achieved through all the numerous efforts made, and despite every concerned person on this earth supposedly having and contributing with different 'good intended ideas and propositions'.

The challenges facing the continent of Africa are so huge that the thought alone sends shivers down my spine.

The legacy of colonial rule, the tribal conflicts and the negative image created, are huge contributing factors to these problems, not forgetting ignorance & corruption.

The pre-colonial and postcolonial times on the continent of Africa brought with it, distinctive differences in the way people, both within and outside of the African continent react to the image that has been created.

The agendas of the European colonial imperialists' invaders onto the African continent, were not hidden, despite the different approaches they used into finally establishing and executing their diabolic plans, whose serious consequences are ever more seen and felt to this day. The 'master and servant' crusade to hold down the locals psychologically, and keep them subservient was put in motion. All efforts were made to break down the existing social structures of the locals, and substituted them with those introduced by the colonial invaders. The locals should be schooled, trained and made to produce for the consumption and benefits of the colonial powers.

The interest of the European imperialists was to overtake the economic and political powers of their colonies. The various kingdoms, empires and tribes on the African continent, had put in place a system of local and foreign trading networks of equal partnership, between themselves and the Europeans. All this changed when the Europeans, cunningly but forcefully, took steps to completely control the natural resources as well as the trade of their various colonies.

The African countries could not achieve success due to the fact that they could not compete with the massive influx of foreign goods from Europe, resulting in the failure of the otherwise hopeful industries they had built.

The European imperialists embarked on an ambitious plan to encourage the growth of cash crops; coffee, cocoa, rubber, timber, and more. Coffee and tea were grown mostly in the colonies from the eastern region whiles cocoa were grown mostly in colonies from the western region of Africa. The European imperial colonial rulers succeeded in making the growth of the different cash crops priorities in their African colonies, in order to meet their own selfish needs. This resulted in those colonies becoming world leaders in the production of the said cash crop, which in turn, had very disastrous consequences for the various African countries, by destroying the many traditional forms of agriculture which catered and supported their local food growth. It became common in some colonies for expatriate farmers to get special treatment, claim the best land, forcing the locals, especially the dark-skin people from sub-Sahara African communities, to work less desirable plots. Unfair treatment of the locals was seen through the introduction of certain rules by some colonial governments, like imposing taxes on the locals from the sub-Saharan African communities. As ways and measures to comply with some of the stringent rules; paying taxes. Many local dark-skin people from the communities in sub-Saharan Africa were forced to abandon their lands, and work for wages on expatriate and white-owned farms and in mines.

Over half a century is gone since many of the African countries who were under the rule of the European imperial colonial powers were emancipated, and achieved their independence from the dreadful colonial rule and have been free to control their political and economic destinies.

The long struggle for independence from the European colonial imperialists by sub-Sahara African countries begun after over 80 years of suppression in every form; suppression from freedom, suppression of the freedom of independent thinking, freedom of self-expression, freedom to make a decision, etc. In reality, how will such a transition be for the sub-Sahara African countries?

The sub-Sahara African communities whose social and political foundations had been by and large, replaced by those introduced by the colonial imperialists invaders over a century, are expected to function as well as the societies in the 'developed countries', or judged by the international community, of whom some are from the same countries that disrupted the foundations of life for the sub-Sahara African communities.

The international community expect without equivocation that "Africans" (really referring to the dark-skin people from the sub-Sahara communities) should do things like they do, think like they think, act like they act, have similar opportunities like they have, and have similar living standards like they do, but can a society that has been through what we know of dark-skin people from sub-Saharan Africa live up to those expectations? It is paradoxical for the international community to have such expectations, I would say.

For the indigenous people, especially of the various communities in sub-Saharan Africa, the situation is very bad in every possible way; the basic living conditions for a majority, the social infrastructures, schools, hospitals,

201

communication, transportation, agriculture, economic conditions, the struggles to be respected and accepted, the daily struggles of survival, the struggle for human equality and recognition, the cultural barriers and traditional challenges, corruption and breakdown of state apparatuses. For the international communities, the complexity of giving the deserved rightful recognition to sub-Sahara African communities after so many decades of looking down on them; treating them as sub-humans, inferior, primitive, letting go of the prejudice, corruption, discrimination, equality, cultural and traditional impediments, can be a serious challenge, after centuries of the era of slavery, colonialism, the pro-colonialism periods, and up the present time.

'Education is the solution,' says many, especially in the 'developed countries'. Is education really the answer to the massive problems facing Africa (referring to the dark-skin communities in sub-Saharan Africa)? Over many years, this seems to be the common suggestion/solution proposed by many who via one way or the other, have cared to give a thought or two. Through the years, the so-called experts on Africa and 'well-wishers', have all indicated and pointed to education as the key to solving the problems of "Africa". A lot has also been done to this effect; several assisting sources in the form of donations from governments, private people, Foundations, organizations and humanitarian organizations around the world, who all continuously contribute financially in various forms towards educating "Africans".

The international news tells of the world-renowned U.S. media personality – Miss Oprah Winfrey, having made efforts in contributing to this notion of educating "Africa" and has personally financed the building of an advanced female-only educational institution in the Republic of South Africa, to enhance the education of females in societies, with special emphasis on those from under-developed societies around the world. Miss Oprah Winfrey has repeatedly made it known of her belief that empowering the females of under-privilege societies is the cornerstone of developing the entire society. In some of the episodes of Miss Oprah Winfrey's then TV Talk-Show – 'The Oprah Show', she often made mention of her belief of the impact of academic education in societies, especially through reading. She is also known for her special interest in reading, which led to her forming a book club, which has grown tremendously over time, and has contributed greatly to the increase of book-readers around the world, more especially in the USA. It is, in my opinion, very easy to understand such contribution from a character like Miss Oprah Winfrey, without being confused about her intent and goals. It is true that by nature, females in societies around the world hold a place in the structuring and growth of their respective communities, if they are not hindered. Their empowerment would definitely have a positive impact on the development of their respective communities, and access to academic education is rightfully a tool for that.

There are references I can think of internationally, the most significant being that proposed and promised by amongst a lot others, The Bill and Melinda Gates Foundation, organizations comprising of wealthy individuals, international foundations, United Nations, OLPC (One Laptop Per Child), several hundred (if not

203

thousands) of various aid and humanitarian organizations and NGOs (non-governmental organizations), all making known of their financial contributions in educating "Africans".

Just like millions of people around the world, I agree that academic education is an important foundation for the positive development of every society. All efforts should be made, and all encouragement and opportunity should be available to the youth of every society, from an early age to get an academic education. As it's often been said and sounding more like a cliché: 'Investing in our children is an investment for our future,' and I am sure all societies around the world would like to do so, including those in sub-Saharan Africa.

It is important to mention that in relation to education in sub-Saharan Africa, it is equally important to shed light on their colonial past, which more than any other factor, has contributed and shaped the state of all the communities who were colonized then, and to the present time.

The languages and educational structures of all the colonized communities had been replaced by those of the colonial imperial governments, which in itself meant that all forms of academic education and schooling were to take place in the language of the colonial powers, as being acceptable. The form of education required then was a serious encroachment on the individual and collective rights of the various colonized communities, much more than the locals were probably aware of. The academic education, as is expected and proposed by many well-wishers and experts for the South-Sahara African communities, consists of many crucial and very challenging factors which need serious consideration. Economic, social, religious, traditional, and cultural factors, are very necessary for the struggle to bring in the key changes needed for the rapid development of the societies in sub-Saharan Africa.

The academic educational system introduced in the sub-Sahara African communities, in my view, was flawed, discriminatory and not accessible to the entire community but to some, especially in the school-going age, which meant that a whole group of people were not included in such a system, and are left behind.

This, in my opinion, gave birth to a massive wave of 'illiteracy' that consumed the entire sub-Saharan Africa region, and especially in the dark-skin population that still exists to this day.

Academic education in sub-Saharan Africa which was introduced in the languages of the colonial invaders, predominantly English, French and Portuguese has done more to widen and create the gaps in the various communities, between the fortunate few, and the unfortunate majority. No matter the advanced forms of social systems existing anywhere in the world, there will still be traces of inequalities which must be attributed to nature, however, that which exists in sub-Saharan Africa, is extreme.

It is without question that the sub-Sahara African countries must heed to the numerous suggestions and advice of educating their citizens, which we know can contribute to reducing the level of suffering, misery, and all the negatives connected to African communities of dark-skin people of countries in sub-Saharan Africa, in every way possible.

Generation after generation have gone through life without their inclusion in the academic education system, leaving many communities in sub-Saharan Africa in very difficult situations which has affected their developments, and led to consequences visible in this present time. The very common worldwide prejudice against dark-skin people from communities in sub-Saharan Africa, and the discrimination against them; looked-down-on, considered primitive and uncultured, daily prevail, in both conscious and sub-conscious ways.

Since it is obvious that it is rather late to get the older generation into any academic education, it is a heavy task for the sub-Saharan African countries to transform their societies by focusing on the children and the coming generation. Introducing academic education to their citizens would involve some significant input on the part of the leaders and the entire societies.

A strong economy is required to finance the educational systems of the various countries down in sub-Saharan Africa, whose economies are shattered, so this will be a serious challenge, amongst others. Academic education in every society requires a good economy, and a better educational system requires an even better economy, so how can these communities achieve better lives?

I personally have a different view on this issue of academic education being the underlining solution to transcend the living standards of dark-skin communities in sub-Sahara Africa.

As controversial as this might appear, I partially disagree with the widely popular opinion that education is the key to solving "Africa's" problems.

No doubt that reading and writing in whichever way, is good for the individual as well as for the society as a whole, in the contribution to development. Absolutely! Where I differ, is the notion that academically educating the population will alter the community in a positive way, but there are no signs of that taking place in the sub-Sahara African communities.

A great percentage of the people from the international communities outside sub-Sahara Africa have no knowledge that many of the countries in sub-Saharan Africa have had formal academic education, contrary to common perception. One significant historical occurrence of the colonial era is the introduction of the form of education in English, French, Portuguese, and the other languages of the colonial governments, which is a testament to the level of education that has transpired in the sub-Sahara African countries. To mention a few, Nigeria, Kenya, Ghana, Zimbabwe, Cote d'Ivoire, Gabon, and many other countries have had very well established pro-colonial and pro-active educational systems as known internationally, especially in Western Europe, resulting in producing academicians and professionals in fields of medicine, engineering, teaching, agriculture, etc.

Since education in any form, should be directly connected to the economies of the societies in sub-Saharan Africa, and it not being a secret about the bad economies of many of these countries, the future of the educated in these same sub-Saharan African countries is understandingly bleak, which in turn directly affects the development of the society.

One does not have to be a rocket scientist to conclude that the continuous exodus of professionals who have had the best education, often provided by the said countries in sub-Saharan Africa; the Teachers, the Doctors, the Engineers, the Planners, the Nurses and the academic elite, will opt for a similar positions elsewhere, if and when provided with a better economic gain than being offered, back in their home countries. The United States of America is a highly developed society who understandably, boasts of the depth of the positive contribution made by migrants, immigrants, and refugees alike, to the building of their society through a couple of centuries, and still does.

I have experienced and heard some of the developed countries (even those with notoriously stringent immigration policies) openly advocating for the recruitment of 'good brains' into their societies, though mostly through a process of selective sorting with the aim of utilizing these 'good brains' to the benefit their societies. These mentioned examples are usually what I refer to as survival of the fittest', with the 'fittest' being the developed countries with the resources to attract and woo the educated from less fortunate countries, like those in sub-Saharan Africa. It is a fact that due to the unfavorable and often, miserable economic conditions, and plus, the influence of the different foreign cultures, especially of Western Europe and North America, via TV and the internet/social media. In various societies in sub-Saharan Africa, academic education, often proposed as being the primary solution to their problems, is not, in my opinion. I dare guarantee that no matter the proposed form of education in sub-Sahara African societies, the temptation to have a better economic position than in their countries of origin, will remain a catalyst for the people, making it enticing for them turning their backs and emigrating to greener pastures, which unfortunately can be anywhere else but their own societies.

'What, then, is the point' I ask, 'is the result of a massive effort to educate people, if the society is not to benefit?'. Due partly to the miserable economies, partly to the exodus of many educated professionals to other countries outside of the sub-Saharan Africa region, and partly due, to the strange habit of looking up to the societies of their former colonial powers in Europe, and North America and plus, the feeling of a better recognition of travels and associations with them.

In comparison with the pre-colonial eras when various societies of dark-skin people in sub-Saharan Africa, had their systems of growth and development; the local education and their forms of social developments that took care of the needy, destroyed and replaced by the systems of the colonial imperialist invaders, the proposals of academic education by many, cannot be the adequate solution, in my opinion. This opinion is by no means a call for non-education but to uphold the traditions and cultures of most of the dark-skin societies in sub-Saharan Africa, which can still positively impact the societies.

I do not think it is wise to conclude that it is primitive for family structures to have kids assisting and helping out with their local family business enterprises to generate positive finances, and form sound economies, which in turn can be good foundations for the families' development, as an alternative to going to school and pursuing academic education, which in its current form in many societies in sub-Saharan Africa, can be arguably unproductive.

This, as I mentioned above, is my personal opinion.

Corruption, corruption, and more corruption, is, like "a cancerous tumor" at the very core of the sub-Saharan African societies that seem to have no cure in sight, despite the extensive diagnoses.

Though I have asked this same question a number of times even in this book, I cannot help but keep asking the same over again: 'How come a continent so blessed with riches in every way, has so much suffering, misery, desperation, poverty, hunger and famine, underdevelopment, disease, and every negative status one can think of?'

Though corruption in communities in sub-Saharan Africa is not exclusive to all other communities around the world, it is a practice which seems to be acceptable as an integral part of the everyday life & thinking, to the detriment of the majority poor & voiceless.

There is no question or doubt whatsoever, that with the rich natural & human resources accessible to almost all the communities in sub-Saharan Africa, their citizens should have access to clean drinking water, access to proper healthcare, access to proper sanitation, access to all forms of education, job creation and access to jobs, so why is that not so?

How do these communities in sub-Saharan Africa who have overseen countless governments struggle with creating environments in which all their citizens benefit from the wealth of the nation, turn things around for more positive transitions into environments that benefits their entire communities, instead of the very few, especially when it's been this way for generations?

Upon careful studies of the political and social systems in most of the dark-skin-populated regions in sub-Saharan Africa, it seems to me (and I could be wrong), that politics is a way to enrich one's self for majority of the politicians, and those who run for influential public positions and offices, due mainly to the lack of accountability and other factors. It is known for a fact, both inside and outside the sub-Sahara African communities, that corruption and embezzlement of state funds is an acceptable act without consequences for the perpetrators, leaving the voiceless, powerless and defenseless people in the communities to pay the terrible price.

I have often said that the resources of the individual communities, belong to each and every citizen of that society, and not for the powerful, manipulative and intimidating few.

The over-exaggerated extent of corruption by the people in power, and the flagrant disregard for the welfare of their fellow citizens, forms the seeds of extreme poverty, which continues to have dire consequences for the existence of the citizens as well as the communities.

There are certain factors directly contributing to the continuous and worsening state of corruption in the sub-Sahara African countries, the most significant in my view, being the traditions existing in these said societies. I know, as I have often been mentioning in this book, the need to cease the generalization relating to the various societies on the African continent, however, certain common traits do exist, especially in the dark-skin communities; the most notable being the role of people's ages in the societies. A very remarkable characteristic noticeable in the dark-skin communities in sub-Saharan Africa, is the respect the elders have in the community; a higher age seems to have an automatic right of respect from the young. As admirable as it is in the cultures and traditions, which have existed and been practiced in all the dark-skin communities in sub-Saharan Africa long before the invasion and colonization of the European Imperialists, there are some negatives, which have direct impacts on the development of the various societies and the undeniable contribution to corruption. How realistic would the crucial transitions from corrupt State and Community Organs into more transparent and accountable state apparatuses be, in the societies?

By the unwritten rules, but via the norms exhibited through the cultures, traditions, and old existing practices, the elders 'hold the answers' in the societies; certainly not the ones younger. Pathetically, this unfortunate culture and tradition, seems to have spilt into the post-colonial era of the political systems, and on to this present day. Equally, the youth are often exempted from decision-making, and having any authority to question the leaders, quashed. The youth, who have been brought up with the same cultures and traditions, do not request for accountability from the elders because it is simply not done; against the norms of tradition, or, in some cases, considered disrespectful. These cultural and traditional systems existing in the dark-skin communities in sub-Saharan Africa, in my humble opinion, has been the leading reason as to the lack of responsibility and accountability, leading to the rapid decay in the social and welfare systems, resulting from corruption.

From everyday experiences, credible sources, and personal interactions with the communities, one can only conclude that the widespread corruption in the dark-skin communities in sub-Saharan Africa has become a serious cultural issue. Every indication points to the fact that it has become acceptable, as well as a way of life for people in positions of authority and power, to assume the 'rights' to access, and freely use the wealth of their countries, for their personal gains, without being accountable to anyone, and showing concern for their communities.

From one government to the next, the dark-skin communities in sub-Saharan Africa, be it democratically elected or by the numerous military interventions, have without shame, been able to act in ways which, in my opinion, are glaring displays of total disrespect for the lives of their citizens. This makes me wonder as to whether such seemingly integrated corrupt behavior, is a legacy passed down from their colonial past. How easy or difficult can a culture which has existed for more than half a century under complete foreign influence, undergo a transition to a more transparent one; having responsible leaders with accountability to their citizens? Many countries in Europe, the Americas, Asia, and elsewhere, have all battled corruption on one level or another in their past, and had to struggle to overcome that era, evolving into the modern and fair societies they enjoy at the present.

A very significant concern I have had regarding the massive uncontrollable corruption levels in the dark-skin communities in sub-Saharan Africa is the obvious status quo in the communities, relating to the demands for their rights to the wealth distribution, individually and collectively.

As common a sight seen internationally, as real it is for the majority of the citizens who suffer daily, from the lack of access to clean drinking water, food, medicine, education, jobs, etc., whiles some people utilize the seemingly unhindered path, to amass huge sums of money objectively, belonging to all citizens of the countries .

As indicated, the widespread level of corruption in the various dark-skin communities in sub-Saharan Africa seems to have become a cultural issue which, in my opinion, can be compared to a malignant and invasive tumor.

When properly diagnosed, all forms of tumor are treated accordingly where necessary, and even more so, aggressively and purposefully, all dependent on the status. So must the widespread corruption in communities in dark-skin sub-Saharan Africa be, but on the contrary, the level and magnitude of the corruption is so pervasive, that it is accepted as a way of life, and a way of doing things.

How does one combat corruption, when it has pervaded every fiber of the society and has been deeply rooted in the thinking of the masses, and embraced?

Corruption, as known, is the number one factor unequivocally detrimental to every form of development in any society.

In reflecting on the ideals of the forefathers from the different dark-skin communities in sub-Saharan Africa who opposed the ideologies of oppressors from outside their borders, freedom and liberty was what they fought and struggled for; however, has that dream and goal been achieved in the development of the societies since formal cessation slavery and colonial rule, and into independence and self-rule? No, it has not, in my opinion!

As pointed out above, when some people, capitalizing on their status as Academicians, Scholars, Elder tribesmen, Politicians, Servicemen and The Military, Religious leaders and the Clergy, Traditional leaders and Authorities in the societies, and disregard the sanctity of what I refer to as 'the law of humanity' – being the love for one's neighbor and ending up unlawfully accessing the country's wealth, and limitlessly enriching themselves without concern for the consequences and effects on the country and the rest of its population, there must be accountability and consequences.

It is beyond my basic human understanding and perception as to how corruption has gained a solid foothold in the societies in sub-Saharan Africa, and seemingly acceptable in the communities. How and why it still is possible in communities, displaying some of the extreme lack of the basic necessities of life; food, clean drinking water, sanitation, health-care, education, etc. I dare claim, with very few exceptions, that all organs of the various governments in the dark-skin population in sub-Saharan Africa, are glaringly corrupt. It is surprising to me that people in positions in society, whose primary duties and obligations are to the welfare of their citizens, often misuses the resources of the countries to their own benefits, and to the bitter detriment of their citizens.

It seems to me, that the easiest pathway to riches in most of the dark-skin populated communities in sub-Saharan Africa, is through politics, or some sort of an influential position in the community, and sadly, rather embraced as an acceptable part of the everyday life. Meanwhile, the extreme suffering in various forms and levels continues.

It has been more of a slogan, often to hear the international community refer to the problems of "Africa" being due to corruption, and the blame often being that of the African leaders. This being partially true, should not go without saying that the international community has to bear part of the blame, as in my opinion, the leaders of the African countries could not succeed in the looting and mismanagement of their countries resources, without their (international community) direct, and indirect contribution. There are many, especially those outside the continent of Africa who might be confused this bold statement I have made, however, upon a devoted interest and comprehension, these people might come to the same conclusion.

In direct reference to situations where large sums of the countries' hard-earned foreign currencies are looted by corrupt leaders and officials, it is seldom that such amounts of monies are kept in the local banks for safe-keeping. Almost always, as if such decisions have some level of prestigious connotation with it, looted, stolen and misappropriated funds are safely kept beyond the borders of the said countries in Africa, but in Europe, The Americas, The Caribbean, The Middle East and Asia. It is without a doubt that such continuous 'milking' of the enormous wealth of the dark-skin communities in sub-

Saharan Africa by their corrupt leaders and officials, can be more attractive and encouraging, via the direct assistance from financial institutions in countries who have since long been acting as safe havens, in aiding and abetting, through their co-operation with these corrupt leaders and officials.

I would say, that there should be equal guilt and accountability with the international community, as it is with those corrupt leaders and officials in sub-Saharan Africa, and should feel responsible for the ensuing dire consequences commonly associated with the dark-skin communities in sub-Saharan Africa.

There should be equal sharing of responsibility, for the demise of every living thing in sub-Saharan Africa, due to the miseries caused by the lack of proper and accountable distribution of the abundance of wealth, and economic resources of the societies.

The international communities' 'hidden assistance' to the corrupt leaders and officials in the dark-skin communities in sub-Saharan Africa, contributing in making it possible for the corruption to be maintained, and grow, should feel 'blood on their hands' for the death and suffering of any child, mother, father, sister, and brother as a result.

Governments, companies and individuals from the international community, who glaringly undertake commitments to co-operate with corrupt leaders and officials from the dark-skin regions in sub-Saharan Africa for their own benefits, knowing that their deeds are borne out of corruption and thereby depriving the innocent and defenseless citizens of some of the basic needs in life, must realize that they are guilty and responsible for the results from the perpetuated 'crimes against humanity' existing daily.

It is beyond belief when one reads and hears about the level and magnitude of the various forms of corruption, and experience what it does to the citizens who live through the effects created.

We are in the 21st century, and one of the most notorious countries on the African continent directly connected with corruption – Nigeria in West Africa, has in their last election, voted in a new government headed by a former military Head of State by name – Muhammad Buhari. He has been on a mission to 'clean up the house' of corruption in their society. In trying to get an idea of the task facing this new government in the fight against corruption, I have seized every opportunity to acquaint myself with the news coming out of Nigeria and some few other countries concerning some of the concrete actions being taken to combat this gigantic 'pestilence'.

A great percentage of the dark-skin societies in sub-Saharan Africa, clearly exhibit extreme forms of poverty unrivaled anywhere else, whiles a few, especially from the older generation, display a massive abundance of wealth and riches. In pondering over this issue, I am baffled as to this seemingly acceptable and even welcoming form of life.

I have often wondered as to why hundreds of thousands of innocent citizens from various communities across sub-Saharan Africa, suffer and die as consequences from lack of basic human needs, whiles the abundance of wealth is exploited and plundered by a few, whiles the world looks on, and even often times, condone such behaviors and practices. It is even a very well recognized perception, that in "Africa", politics is a means to wealth and riches.

Some of these stories of excessive and out-of-control corruption and mismanagement relating to leaders and people in authority from dark-skin communities in sub-Saharan Africa are simply astonishing, and incomprehensive. Some of these stories one hears about in different forms, be it authentic or exaggerated are so detrimental to the lives and growth of the masses of their innocent citizens, who are openly deprived of the basic necessities of life. In fairness, being corrupt and squandering the wealth and resources of various countries in sub-Saharan Africa are not acts usually warranting accountability and consequences for the actors, thereby making it difficult to question such acts deemed unethical to the outside world, if to most people in such communities, it is 'acceptable' and 'normal'.

Notorious and common traits of corruption in the dark-skin communities in sub-Saharan Africa by people in authority can be cited in various forms; political leaders (presidents, prime ministers and other ministers, heads of state, military leaders and other people in political positions of authority) in The Democratic Republic of Congo (formerly Zaire), Nigeria, Central African Republic, Ghana, Cote d'Ivoire, Senegal, Ethiopia, Uganda, Zambia, Tanzania, Republic of Togo, Republic of Benin, Chad Republic, Republic of Niger, Republic of South Africa, and more, have (through substantiative reports), openly and covertly stashed state funds and valuables in and out of their countries. Known information (some fictional and others authentic) of secret international bank accounts, both at home and abroad belonging to people in political and social power, is common amongst the populace.

Gold, diamonds, crude oil, copper, bauxite, manganese, timber, rubber, agricultural-produce, diverse valuable rare earth elements like minerals, metals, coltan (a metallic ore consisting of columbite and tantalite), and other valuable products that nature has given to humanity and to these various communities in sub-Saharan Africa, constituting the bedrock of any rich and blessed society, and which should be to the benefit of their citizens, has been a buffet of massive wealth to these corrupt leaders, who willingly and uncontrollably serve themselves.

I dare say that in far many instances, these corrupt leaders in the various societies are morally, consciously and ethically bankrupt, to say the least.

In Ghana as well as in many other countries in sub-Saharan Africa, there are series of documented cases of complete degeneration of communities; no basic drinking water and basic food leading to malnutrition; zero health system, leading to commonly preventable diseases & senseless deaths; breakdown of the basic educational system, depriving the communities of growth & future developments; the complete breakdown of social systems, depriving people of their welfare and leading to widespread apathy amongst the majority, all this whiles the minority few plunder the vast rich resources of the communities, which are more than enough to solve most of the problems aforementioned here.

I have often wondered if there is any greater sin against humanity than this openly displayed corruption in its worst forms.

In reflecting over some of the points raised, I cannot withstand the urge to mention, or repeat that dark-skin politicians in sub-Saharan African societies go into politics not to utilize the platforms to serve their people and better their lives, but rather to enrich themselves. What I find grotesque about this seemingly permanent way of life, is that these corrupt political leaders as well as people in authority, do not shy away from these practices, but rather, display acts of slightly bizarre conspicuous modus operandi in their attitudes.

I am of the opinion that a person in society, or a politician elected into office, adheres to a pledge (written or unwritten) to serve the very same people who elected him or her, unless I am thinking in an extremely conservative and archaic way; however, my observation is that people in political power as well as other forms of authority in societies in sub-Saharan Africa, do get served, over-served and expect to be served by the electorate. In many instances, current and historically, depictions of leaders in dark-skin sub-Saharan African societies have either presented themselves as demi-gods, or, been treated so by their citizens, either through force and intimidation, or by other means necessary to uphold such status, discarding and disregarding the rule of law, and proper governance.

"Africa" (the common reference to the dark-skin people from the African continent), the continent synonymous with corrupt political leaders, extreme poverty, hopelessness, degradation and misery, has a stereo-type image known to the entire world. Meanwhile, the exorbitant and lavish lifestyles of these corrupt leaders, stemming from the colossal level of corruption,

221

looting, mismanagement of State and national resources, continues unchallenged.

Though through the struggles of their forefathers, democracy, as it should be understood, has come to bear on the entire continent and yet, we see time and again that these leaders and their cohorts continue to disregard the same democratic values for which they have campaigned and ascended onto the 'throne of power' by fair or foul means. Often as history has depicted, there have been countless military coups and interventions which replaces elected governments, often leaving trails of blood and tragic encounters and consequences involving innocent civilians, and not leading to life improvements for their citizens in question. On the contrary, there are many documented cases where things have gone on to be far worse than before, as typically, these military leaders themselves become stooges of the corrupt system and the misuse of the countries' financial resources and eventually, as it's usually is, becoming an addition to the never-ending compilation of statistics and numbers.

Often, in their seemingly hard efforts to abide by, and practice the rule-of-law, most of these indisciplined corrupt leaders and their stooges in dark-skin populations in sub-Saharan Africa, resort to the blatant disregard for democratic elections to bring changes.

There are daily documentations across the sub-Saharan African continent where all efforts to derail the democratic systems in place are a familiar occurrence, all for the retaining of their governmental powers and the continuous rule. The one-ballot, one-vote rule as known in all democratic systems throughout history is usually cast aside and disregarded, and all so often, openly infringing on the human rights of their citizens.

In recent months, there has been some highly anticipated General Elections in some sub-Saharan African countries notably Uganda, Gambia, Ghana and unfortunately but unsurprisingly, in two out of these 3 situations, serious disputes have been dominating the outcome, usually leading to challenges of the results by the incumbent government. Often, the incumbent government finds one way or the other to present reasons for disputes that can drag on for lengthy periods with serious uncertainties as part of the consequences for the population.

In sub-Saharan Africa, though less visible and felt today than in previous times, many leaders have clung and still cling to power and refuse to relinquish it. It is not an exaggeration to conclude that certain leaders have been in power for close to a third of a lifespan and do not show signs of giving over power to others. It is obvious why some of these leaders decide to stay so long in power, considering some of the catalysts as described above.

We are experiencing the end of the year 2016, and there is an international effort to get the long-term President of the Republic of Gambia – Yahya Jammeh, who, as many others in sub-Saharan Africa throughout the years, seized power in 1994 through a military coup and has remained in power through a 4-year-term election period – in 3 successive elections. The man is doing all he can to stay in power despite him losing (according to the Gambians themselves and international observers) to his main opponent. He consequently agreed, initially, (reluctantly) to accept the results and the outcome of the election, only to rescind this decision a while later. The Gambian populous, the United Nations (UN), the African Union (AU) and the leaders of the Economic Community of West African States (ECOWAS) have all made efforts to convince this Gambian president to accept the verdict and step down for the winner to take over, but he remains defiant and adamant. This, as often is the case, leads into unwarranted internal opposition through uprising, demonstrations, and eventual bloodshed, which results in the loss of innocent lives.

Meanwhile, a similar situation is manifesting itself across the African continent to the central-eastern part in the Republic of DR Congo (formerly known as Congo-Kinshasa), whose president – Mr. Joseph Kabila – is surprisingly ignoring the constitution of the same country he is the government leader of, by not addressing the date for the elections for a new term, for reasons better known to himself and his supporters. I know for a fact that Mr. Joseph Kabila took over power after succeeding his father in a line of former presidents. His father – Mr. Laurent Kabila – was assassinated by one of his own bodyguards in the year 2001 after he himself had overthrown another notorious President Mobutu Sese Seko. It is worth noting that the current president – Mr. Joseph Kabila – succeeded his father – Mr. Laurent Kabila – just eight days after his assassination. As expected, there have been some reactions by protesters in the country, which has led to some unrest and consequently the loss of lives. The status is that the political and civilian state of affairs remains tense.

Something similar could be said about the East African country of Uganda whose current leader was involved in a similar general election dispute, which (according to news out of Uganda) involved the arrest and subsequent detention of one of the main opposition leaders who was questioning the legitimacy of the election process vis-à-vis the results in which the incumbent president, Yoweri Museveni - who has been in power for approximately 30 years, was declared a winner.

In summarizing, there is a question which I have often asked myself, and so has many others from different countries from the African continent and elsewhere, which is: 'Why is it often so that the leaders, especially from dark-skin populated regions in sub-Saharan Africa, do not want to respect the constitutions of their sovereign nations and the democratic principles for which they have sworn to protect...why?'

There are many guesses as to reasons why, from many of us no matter the wide differences, however, we all agree on one thing, which is, that nobody can claim to have the answers to the real reason why these political leaders seem to want to govern for as long as they can. What makes these politicians behave as if they own the countries which they lead?

In the on-going political upheaval regarding the West African country of Gambia, I have, to my positive surprise, read various reviews and reactions to the seemingly unsurprised (based on the standards exhibited by many sub-Saharan African country leaders over so many years) repeated behaviors, however, the tone is different. It seems to me that people originating especially from sub-Saharan African countries, have a different view to these abominable repeated attitudes of these sub-Saharan African countries leaders and thereby not holding back on their condemnation, criticisms, and defiant cries for immediate change, unlike before.

A friend of mine sent me a short video recording of a session from a church service in a black church somewhere here in the US, where the pastor giving that sermon was being very emphatic about a particular subject, which had to do with how he – pastor, felt the need to let all know about 'black people having a serious problem', and that 'all had to pray seriously to God for some intervention, and to bring a change in the way of their thinking, and relating actions'. This pastor had a 'Ph.D.' degree to his name, which to me, and I am sure many others, indicates some sense of high-level studies of a particular educational subject. In short, I will not be far off if my conclusion on this pastor's credentials must contain some level of intelligence.

In an act of seriousness, this pastor utters in a raised voice synonymous with the way certain 'gifted Orators present their messages, telling the congregation that he believed that black people have a problem which needs to be seriously addressed, as well as needing serious prayers.

His point was that wherever black people had had, or been given the opportunity to self-govern, it has been disastrous and without the slightest hesitation, this pastor makes a direct reference to "Africa"!

'Look at Africa,' he emphasized with a high deep voice, 'they have done nothing constructive, or built anything worth showing for,' he went on ranting.

'All they have out there are huts built out of clay and wood, and nothing of quality engineering worth referring to.'

'The worst thing that could happen to the Africans was when the White folks handed power over to Mr. Mandela,' he said.

'Look at what is happening there in South Africa, they are killing each other, black people have a very serious problem,' he added.

In a show of ignorance often displayed by people who have no clue whatsoever on the African Continent and its people and not showing any interest to learn, he went on boastfully stating (in sought of a reaction to his own narration), 'Yes, I know, that Egypt built the pyramids and civilization started from there and all, I know that but Egypt is not Africa,' he added.

In the display of ignorance from an 'educated' black man with roots from sub-Saharan Africa being a catalyst for my bringing this up in this chapter, the real reason is to make reference to South Africa, in direct relation to the theme mentioned above, and to do with the President of the Republic of South Africa – Mr. Jacob Zuma.

It should not go without saying that in all fairness and in memory of the late president of South Africa – Mr. Nelson Mandela, who was also seen and regarded by many of the blacks in Southern Africa as a man of honor and dignity – that the incumbent president is a pale shadow of an example of the kind of leadership quality shown by Mr. Mandela, in the pursuit for a change from corrupt governance, to one that can impact a positive on the lives of the many suffering people.

The multiple scandalous stories surrounding the incumbent South African president – Mr. Jacob Zuma – is simply appalling. Politically, socially, integrity-wise – statesmanship and credibility; he seems to have lost it all, even amongst his party faithful and internationally. Credible stories of massive corruption and misuse of funds belonging to the State. Sporadic stories involving blatant disregard for the stipulations of the constitution for which he is a chosen guardian. When will these unfortunate but hurtful actions that seem to be the normality with leaders in sub-Saharan African countries cease to exist, and wishfully eradicated?

This brings me back to the question I have asked above, having to do with the possible reason as to why the leaders in dark-skin populated countries in sub-Saharan Africa seems to be ruthless in their pursuit of actions detrimental to the positive growth and happiness of their people.

In reflecting on the stories (documented and undocumented) regarding the magnitude of corruption involving the leaders in dark-skin populated countries in sub-Saharan Africa, and the seemingly out-of-control greed with which this atrocity is perpetrated, I cannot help but wonder, just like many do, as to the reason behind it all. This question, as appropriately direct as it might seem, is to me, more of an instinctive reaction to what I, along with many others, have been struggling to deal with. What would make someone who has all intended purposes to divert by foul means, the hard-earned monies belonging to a whole community, be so greedy and inconsiderate to a level unimaginable?

Corruption is not a phenomenon solely reserved for African societies (as is the thinking tendencies of many people) but is experienced in practically all other societies around the world. The difference, in my opinion, is the implementation of various legislations in different societies around the world in combating this menace to all forms of development in society, and the proper enforcement of the measures of consequences in dealing with it, put in place.

The underlining difference, in my opinion, is the fact that unlike the measures put in place in the developed societies where various forms of corruption have consequences, plus, the rule of law being enforced, it is the opposite in the sub-Saharan African societies.

The foundations of these sub-Saharan African societies are riddled with incompetence at all levels within the justice system, making the enforcement of the various rules put in place very fragile and not respected.

Leaders and people in positions of authority have given themselves the right to be corrupt, knowing that there are no demands for accountability from them, and no consequences either. Winds of the acceptability of such malpractices have for years been blowing in these societies, leading directly to the abominable states that they have been in, and are still in.

The disgraceful outcome of the presidential elections in the Gambia is an example in this modern era.

After openly refusing to accept defeat and relinquishing his post as president despite several appellation and intervention by the United Nations, some from the international community, as well as from the leaders from the ECOWAS (the West African Economic

Community) for many weeks, and creating a sense of a serious political stand-off with his citizens, and those who had intended to intervene, Mr. Yahya Jammeh finally decided to give in and apparently accept an offer to go into exile. It is widely reported in the media that in his flight out of his country, he managed to loot a huge sum of money and other property belonging to his nation, which he took with him out of the country.

I am extremely curious to know whether there will be any consequences for such blatant disregard and lack of respect for a society that he once lead.

I once heard a wise man state that, quote: 'Power corrupts, and absolute power corrupts absolutely,' unquote. This quotation gives so much meaning to the sickening level of corruption in the sub-Saharan African societies. This is more so when it is always evident that in the various degrees of corruption, one sees or hears of the struggle for power.

All across sub-Saharan Africa, this practice has been on-going for decades on, without any sign of it subsiding. Rather, the level of corruption is as strong as it's ever been, if not even more.

In some of the sporadic discussions I have had with some of my acquaintances, and strangers as well, concerning amongst others, this specific topic, it does not surprise me with their diverse opinions and suggestions, which are far and few in between. One sure significant conclusion from these various discussions, is the fact that, the problem of corruption, abuse of power, and mismanagement by the leaders, of their various countries' resources whiles their citizens suffer in utmost negative conditions known to man, is well known to all of them. The conclusions of many who show interest are also very diverse, with no specific proclamation of the best solution. My question is, why?

Reasons are given, implying the sacrifice of one's life through the often known methods; the use of brutal force by these corrupt leaders in fortifying their positions in power, and resulting in bloodshed and loss of lives. This seems to be a dilemma for the majority of concerned citizens.

What then could be the reason the 'developed countries' seem not to do much about this particular situation?

Could it be the concern of these developed countries not to be seen to interfere in the affairs of other nations? This cannot be, as it has never been a hidden fact, that they ('developed countries'), do get involved in other countries' 'business' for one reason or the other. I would again claim here, of some other possible reasons which, in my opinion, can be a dilemma.

Through my little research in writing this book, I have come to define what I refer to as the three major causes and factors contributing to the sorry state of "Africa" – the dark-skin regions in sub-Saharan Africa, and are:

1. IGNORANCE
2. CORRUPTION and POWER STRUGGLE
3. EDUCATION

Ironically, these are factors which also unquestionably, plays a role in the status quo, from both the sub-Saharan Africa societies, as well as the international community in their actions concerning "Africa".

In the modern day international relationships in which diplomacy is the key to building and maintaining strong bonds between various nations, whiles respecting other nations' sovereign rights, could that create a sensitive factor in confronting the problems and issues which are, and can be, clear reasons for the said situations in various sovereign African countries?

My biggest dream and hope is that a time will come in the not too distant future, where people all over the world will learn to recognize and embrace the differences and diversities of the dark-skin people from societies in sub-Saharan Africa, without malice and discrimination, and treat them with equality, respect and human dignity.

Would the world be ready to confront injustice to the less fortunate, and make way for indiscriminate paths to development for all, with less regard for the foreseen political and economic consequences that might interfere?

Will there be room for tolerance of all dark-skin people from sub-Sahara Africa, and, will people finally learn to uphold and display their differences, and do away with the common misconception of all Africans being one people with one language from a country known as "Africa?" The day when people from the country of Kenya will be known a Kenyans, as would those from Nigeria be known as Nigerians, and those from Zambia known as Zambians, and so on.